THE WRITER'S GARDEN

THE WRITER'S GARDEN

How gardens inspired our best-loved authors

F

FRANCES LINCOLN LIMITED
PUBLISHERS

Jackie Bennett
Photography by Richard Hanson

Frances Lincoln Ltd
A subsidiary of Quarto Publishing Group UK
74–77 White Lion Street
London N1 9PF

The Writer's Garden
Copyright © Frances Lincoln Ltd 2014
Text copyright © Jackie Bennett 2014
Photographs copyright © Richard Hanson 2014

First Frances Lincoln edition 2014
First Frances Lincoln paperback edition 2016

A catalogue record for this book is available from the British Library

ISBN 978-0-7112-3840-4

Printed in China

9 8 7 6 5 4 3 2 1

Quarto is the authority on a wide range of topics.

Quarto educates, entertains and enriches the lives of
our readers – enthusiasts and lovers of hands-on living.

www.QuartoKnows.com

HALF-TITLE The front door leads straight on to the garden at Thomas
Hardy's Cottage in Higher Bockhampton.
TITLE PAGES Near Sawrey in the Lake District is the village in which Beatrix
Potter made her home.
RIGHT Virginia Woolf's writing hut is to be found at the edge of the
orchard at Monk's House, Rodmell.

Contents

Introduction   6

Jane Austen at Godmersham and Chawton   10

Rupert Brooke at Grantchester   20

John Ruskin at Brantwood   28

Agatha Christie at Greenway   36

Beatrix Potter at Hill Top   44

Roald Dahl at Gipsy House   54

Charles Dickens at Gad's Hill Place   62

Virginia Woolf at Monk's House   68

Winston Churchill at Chartwell   76

Laurence Sterne at Shandy Hall   84

George Bernard Shaw at Shaw's Corner   92

Ted Hughes at Lumb Bank   98

Henry James *followed by* E.F. Benson at Lamb House   106

John Clare at Helpston   114

Thomas Hardy at Hardy's Cottage and Max Gate   120

Robert Burns at Ellisland   130

William Wordsworth at Cockermouth and Grasmere   138

Walter Scott at Abbotsford   148

Rudyard Kipling at Bateman's   158

Garden Visiting Information   168

Sources of Quotes   170

Further Reading   172

Index   172

Acknowledgments   176

Introduction

'The garden is the place I go to for refuge and shelter, not the house . . . there . . . I feel protected and at home, and every flower and weed is a friend.'

ELIZABETH VON ARNIM, 1898

Gardens hold a special place in many writer's lives. Novelists, poets, biographers and authors of children's books, from Agatha Christie to Rupert Brooke, Beatrix Potter to Henry James, have turned to gardens for inspiration – their own and those that they knew best.

Great things happen in gardens – in fiction as in real life. No one reading Daphne du Maurier's *Rebecca* could doubt that the author herself had lived with the huge, blood-red rhododendrons that the heroine first sees on arrival at Manderley. Roald Dahl's close study of his own fruit trees in his Buckinghamshire garden gave him the idea for *James and the Giant Peach*. Virginia Woolf wove the gardens she knew into all her stories, from *Kew Gardens* to *Mrs Dalloway*, while Agatha Christie hardly bothered to disguise her beloved house – Greenway – and its garden, which appeared in several of her crime novels. And, where would Jane Austen's characters have walked, talked and schemed if their creator had never seen a Wilderness or a Shrubbery?

Some writers, such as the poets Robert Burns and John Clare, were born into rural families who worked the land, but for others the joy of making a garden came later in their lives. For Beatrix Potter at Hill Top Farm and Sir Walter Scott at Abbotsford, creating a garden was made possible only by the new-found freedom and wealth brought about by their literary success. Massachusetts poet Emily Dickinson was probably better known for her Amherst garden than her poetry – at least during her lifetime – and novelist H.E. Bates, the creator of *The Darling Buds of May*, wrote several gardening books later in his career.

In *The Writer's Garden* the featured writers emerge from very different backgrounds. Thomas Hardy was raised in rural Dorset, where he collected cider apples for the annual pressing and relied on the vegetable plot at the family's thatched cottage to supply food. Sir Winston Churchill, on the other hand, grew up at Blenheim Palace, with its 'Capability' Brown landscapes and capacious lakes. Yet, when both men reached maturity and were in a position to create their own gardens, they threw themselves back into the past – into their childhood years. Hardy tried to be almost self-sufficient at Max Gate in Dorchester, while Churchill hired a digger to enlarge his lakes at Chartwell, in an attempt to elevate them from 'pond' to 'lakes' – and so closer to those at Blenheim.

The Writer's Retreat

Gardens have also provided writers with solace – a place to escape to, to think and to write. The 'writer's retreat' is an enduring image that many of us try to recreate in our own gardens. The ultimate such retreat must be Dylan Thomas's cliff-top writing shed at the Boathouse in Laugharne; for many people, it still represents the perfect hideaway. Mark Twain's cabin in California, where he sketched out ideas for *The Celebrated Jumping Frog of Calaveras County*, has taken on an almost mythical status. The hut that Henry David Thoreau built for himself, at Walden Pond, has become an important icon for those wanting to get into the mindset of the man who lived in the woods for two years to prepare for his great work, *Walden*. And the enigmatic and ultimately tragic life of Virginia Woolf has meant that her simple, wooden writing 'lodge' at Monk's House has

become something of a shrine. Roald Dahl, George Bernard Shaw and Charles Dickens also found it essential to work in a quiet place and so retreated to a 'shed' in the garden, away from the distractions of the house.

A Gardener's Calling

Most of the writers in this book employed gardeners, but that is not to say that they were not hands-on themselves, when time allowed. Scott was a great tree planter – as was Hardy, who planted 2,000 Austrian pines at Max Gate. Churchill would don his boiler suit and go out into the grounds at Chartwell to rebuild the walls in the Kitchen Garden. Charles Dickens would walk around his garden in Kent every morning, tools in hand, mending anything that needed repair; and Beatrix Potter spent many hours planting gifts from neighbours.

OPPOSITE The boathouse at Agatha Christie's Greenway, in Devon, was the atmospheric setting used in several of her crime novels.

ABOVE Author Mark Twain spent the winter of 1864–5 in a wood cabin on Jackass Hill, California, where he got the idea for his first story.

LEFT For the last four years of his life, Dylan Thomas worked from a cliff-top shed at the Boathouse, in Laugharne on the south-west coast of Wales.

Every gardener knows how easy, and often desirable, it is to 'lose oneself' in the garden. One of the most captivating books on this theme is *Elizabeth and Her German Garden*. Published anonymously in 1898, it is a fictionalized account of the author, Elizabeth von Arnim – a young English woman newly married to a Prussian aristocrat. While she is supposed to be overseeing the papering and painting of their enormous house, she instead spends an idyllic few months alone, exploring the wild garden and having her meals brought to her on a tray outdoors: 'I lived in a world of dandelions and delights . . . the lawns have long since blossomed out into meadows filled with every sort of pretty weed – and under and among the . . . oaks and beeches were blue hepaticas, white anemones, violets, and celandines in sheets.' When she does, occasionally, remember that she has a husband, von Arnim is pricked by conscience, but it does nothing to lessen the discovery of true love . . . her garden.

Gardens Lost and Found

In many ways, we are extraordinarily lucky to have so many writers' gardens. Writers, particularly those struggling in the early stages of their career, tend to be itinerant by nature and therefore unlikely to settle, or to make a garden. Those gardens that do exist had often had a narrow escape – in 1937, Wordsworth's birthplace at Cockermouth was nearly pulled down before being saved by local people. Other houses were not so fortunate. Enid Blyton's home, Green Hedges, known to children all over the world (the name itself was chosen by her young readers when she moved there in 1938) was demolished in the 1970s; no trace of it remains. The poet Percy Bysshe Shelley's Boscombe House, in Bournemouth, is now a medical centre; and the Berkshire house near the river Thames, where Kenneth Grahame stayed as a boy with his grandmother and which inspired *The Wind in the Willows*, is now a school.

The one 'lost' garden that captures the imagination more than any other is *The Secret Garden*, invented by Frances Hodgson Burnett. Her timeless story of a sick boy and an orphaned girl who find happiness in an overgrown walled garden has never lost its appeal. The house and garden thought to have inspired it – or where Hodgson Burnett was living when she wrote *The Secret Garden* – is Great Maytham Hall. Now a private residential development, it is equally as grand as Misselthwaite Manor, even if the location is in leafy Kent rather than the wild moorlands of Yorkshire. If nothing can ever quite match the magic of an imaginary garden, at least Great Maytham Hall still exists.

There is something even more magical about lost gardens that are 'found'. In the 1870s, a thirteen-year-old boy came to live in Dumfries to be educated at the Dumfries Academy. His name was James Barrie – better known as J.M. Barrie – and he and his brother would spend their free time playing at a big Georgian town house, Moat Brae, which was owned by the Gordon family. Later in life, Barrie remembered how happy he was there and talked about the 'enchanted land', alluding to the fact that this was where he had had the idea for *Peter Pan*. Moat Brae is far grander than Barrie's own birthplace in Kirriemuir, where he was one of seven children, and it is easily imaginable as the home of the Darling children. It had gardens that ran down to the river and its wild, wooded riverbank certainly enchanted the young Barrie, and stayed with him all his life.

In 2009 Moat Brae was saved from the bulldozer with just a few days before the deadline. Since then, the Peter Pan Moat Brae Trust has worked tirelessly to raise funds internationally to turn the house into a Centre for Children's Literature. The aim is to re-invent, rather than recreate, the gardens – turning them into a living place for children to learn through play, very much in the spirit of *Peter Pan*.

Living Places

Gardens are not static objects like old china or furniture, which might only need an occasional dust. They grow quickly, and they change. Sir Walter Scott's Abbotsford, where one man imagined, designed and then created his unique vision, was fortunate in being cared for by a succession of descendants who understood its story. Other gardens such as John Ruskin's Brantwood are still being decoded and will continue to be an exciting voyage of discovery for their caretakers. This book pays tribute to the owners, curators and gardeners who keep them going. If there is such a thing as a writer's spirit, then it lives on through the people who renew that spirit, year after year.

OPPOSITE Enid Blyton enjoyed working in her garden at Green Hedges in Beaconsfield, Buckinghamshire, where she moved in 1938.
BELOW TOP LEFT As a child, J.M. Barrie played in the garden at Moat Brae, Dumfries, which gave him the inspiration for Peter Pan.
BELOW TOP RIGHT Brantwood, the home of the artist, writer and social commentator John Ruskin, lies on the shores of Coniston Water in the Lake District.
BELOW BOTTOM LEFT Sir Walter Scott created his spectacular castle at Abbotsford, in the Scottish Borders, and designed the walled gardens in a complementary style.
BELOW BOTTOM RIGHT The garden created by Beatrix Potter at Hill Top was featured in several of her illustrated children's stories.

Jane Austen at Godmersham and Chawton

'. . . before she had been five minutes within its walls . . . she quitted it again, stealing away through the winding shrubberies, now just beginning to be in beauty, to gain a distant eminence.'

SENSE AND SENSIBILITY

There is a widely held image of Jane Austen as a well-to-do, young woman who did nothing more arduous than a little embroidery or flower arranging. It is surprising how pervasive this thinking is – even if it is the characters in her novels who have given this impression, rather than the woman herself.

In fact, Jane knew a good deal about gardens and gardening. She was born into a learned but not at all privileged family – her father was the rector of the poor rural parish of Steventon in Hampshire, and her home from birth was the shambolic, but happy, rectory. Jane's father farmed the land around, growing crops and raising cattle and, to make up the family income, taught a group of boys who lived with the family in term time. Her mother helped to run the school as well as manage their self-sufficient smallholding with its dairy and garden for growing vegetables.

Jane and her sister Cassandra, who was a couple of years older, would have had a boisterous childhood, when they were expected to help with the chores. The household brewed its own beer, made butter and kept cows to be milked, and Jane would have fed the chickens in the poultry yard and taken water to the animals. When haymaking time came round, she and Cassandra – along with her elder brothers James, Edward, Henry and Charles – were expected to help. It was a childhood steeped in rural rhythms in which Jane took pony rides, walked through muddy lanes and would have naturally absorbed knowledge about the seasons and harvests. It was also a place full of laughter, and at the back of the house there was a green slope down which the children would roll. In the garden, there were flowers – for cutting mainly – and strawberry beds for picking, under the close eye of Mrs Austen.

Sadly, the rectory is the one Jane Austen garden we cannot see – the house was pulled down in 1823 by her brother Edward, and only fields remain. It dominated her formative years, provided her underlying stability and was the place in which as a young woman she wrote the drafts of her first three novels: 'First Impressions', 'Elinor and Marianne' and 'Susan' – later to become, respectively, *Pride and Prejudice, Sense and Sensibility* and *Northanger Abbey*.

Around Steventon there lived several landed gentry, who were the Austens' neighbours. The Austens never had much money compared with their contemporaries, but the knowledge of these grander houses fed Jane's imagination. She would have known

RIGHT The Austens' Rectory in the village of Steventon, Hampshire is where Jane Austen spent her childhood.
OPPOSITE Jane's brother Edward lived at Godmersham Park, Kent from 1797.

of Hurstbourne Park – the grandest one and home of Lord Portsmouth and of the many scandals that surrounded him. She certainly visited Manydown, home of the Bigg family, and it was at a ball there that Jane *possibly* accepted a proposal from Tom Lefroy, the young lawyer whom she had fallen in love with. The Chutes, who lived at The Vyne, were a grander family than the Austens, but their lives connected at many points. Jane would have known how such people lived, and it is this contrast – between her own home with its working garden and the lives of those on large estates – that makes her work so rich and multilayered.

The brief encounter with Tom Lefroy left a deep impression on Jane – it was to be her only true affair of the heart. But, as neither family had resources, they were never to be united. The fortunes of her brother Edward, meanwhile, were taking an unexpected upturn. He was adopted by the Knights – a wealthy, distantly related family, who were childless and needed a male heir. He went on to inherit several estates including Godmersham Park in Kent. Jane and Cassandra were regular visitors there from Steventon and stayed for the summers of 1794 and 1796. In 1797 Edward and his new wife Elizabeth went to live there permanently. Jane remarked humorously to Cassandra that 'Kent is the only place for happiness – everybody is rich there.'

Godmersham Park

Jane had seen many grand houses and gardens in Hampshire, but the beauty and space of her brother's home at Godmersham was still impressive. She wrote to Cassandra from there in June 1808: '. . . Yesterday passed quite à la Godmersham: the gentlemen rode about Edward's farm and returned in time to saunter along Bentigh [the lime avenue] with us; and after dinner we visited the Temple Plantations . . .'

The gardens of 10 hectares / 24 acres consisted of two linking walled gardens, a Wilderness and two classical temples – one with a clear vista of the south facade of the house, the other out in the wider park, just a walk across fields via a little bridge over the river Stour. In the late eighteenth century a Wilderness such as that at Godmersham Park would have been more formal than the name suggests and would have had yew hedges and secluded walks.

Godmersham had all the components of a great eighteenth-century estate, and it is not difficult to imagine how Jane would have enjoyed getting away from the hurly-burly of Edward's household (growing quickly – he had eleven children in all) to read or write or just think her own thoughts within the walled grounds. There was even a door in the wall that allowed the residents to access the village church on Sundays. It is now known in the garden as the Mr Collins's door – after the sycophantic clergyman in *Pride and Prejudice*.

The gardens today do not just reflect the Jane Austen era. The walled gardens were remodelled in the 1930s by the great designer Norah Lindsey, and an Italian Garden and a Swimming Pool Garden were added to reflect the interests of that age. One of the walled gardens, probably used for stabling in the eighteenth century, is now a pretty Rose Garden. The original Lime Tree Avenue (which Jane would have known as Bentigh) was devastated in the storms of 1987 and replanted in the 1990s. Among the great features of the garden are the topiary hedging and, in spring, the carpets of narcissi and *Anemone blanda* beneath flowering fruit trees.

For Jane, Godmersham was a richly interesting place to visit, but it was never home. In 1801 her father retired from the living at Steventon, and the family moved out of the rectory to make way for

One of the classical temples at Godmersham lies at the end of the Wilderness.

OPPOSITE This woodcut engraving of Jane Austen (1775–1817), which hangs in Jane Austen's House Museum in Chawton, is taken from a late nineteenth-century painting commissioned by Jane Austen's nephew James Edward Austen-Leigh and is based on memories of his aunt.

ABOVE LEFT One of the classical temples at Godmersham lies at the end of the Wilderness.

BELOW LEFT The Lime Tree Avenue was originally planted by Jane's brother Edward, in a field known as Bentigh. Those trees were damaged in the storm of 1987, and the avenue has since been replanted. The family would have walked down the avenue to reach the village church.

her eldest brother James. What followed for Jane was catastrophic in terms of her emotional and literary development, and she would write little for the next eight years. In 1805 the Reverend Austen died, and, as his legacy was meagre, Jane, Cassandra and their mother were thrown on the goodwill of the brothers. They moved about constantly, spending their winters in a series of rented houses in Bath and their summers with relatives.

Their travels from one brother to another, and to a series of country estates of distant relatives, must have exposed Jane to the great contrasts between cottagers, who gardened for their subsistence and pleasure, and the more comfortably off, who had the means to 'improve' their land. She was well versed in the arguments about landscape gardens, and she is known to have visited Adlestrop in Gloucestershire, where she was shown the work of Humphry Repton, and Stoneleigh in Warwickshire, with its abbey ruins, large Kitchen Garden and Chapel in the grounds, which almost certainly found its way into *Mansfield Park*.

But her own reality was a house in Southampton, shared with her naval brother Frank and his wife. Jane, long divorced from having her own garden, seized on this one adjoining the town walls and wrote excitedly about buying lilac, laburnum and currant bushes to plant. But she disliked town life, and when Edward suggested they spend the summer holidays of 1807 at Chawton House in her home county of Hampshire she jumped at the chance – her first visit to the village that would be her home for the rest of her life.

Return to Hampshire

Chawton House, its estate village and farmland came to Edward as part of the Knight inheritance – he would eventually take his benefactor's name and become Edward Knight. Jane longed for somewhere to settle, and Edward offered his mother and sisters a choice between a cottage near Godmersham and the recently vacated bailiff's cottage on the Chawton estate. Mrs Austen preferred Kent, but Jane, now thirty-three years old, was convinced that Chawton was the place. She won, and four women – Mrs Austen, Jane, Cassandra and their friend Martha Lloyd – moved there in July 1809.

The cottage (now known as Jane Austen's House Museum) was actually a substantial house with six bedrooms, situated right in

the centre of the village, a short walk from the 'big house'. It was perhaps closest to Barton Cottage – the house in Devon that Elinor and Marianne move to in *Sense and Sensibility* – although Jane had written the first draft of this novel many years earlier. At the time it was probably 1 hectare/2½ acres or so – larger than the current garden – and certainly had an orchard, beehives, a Kitchen Garden (which Mrs Austen looked after) and a Shrubbery – the essential feature of an early nineteenth-century garden. It was screened from the road by a wooden fence and a hornbeam hedge (now a wall), and there was space for the Austens to walk around the perimeter under the shade of trees. There was long grass 'to mow', and a Gravel Walk.

LEFT ABOVE This watercolour of the cottage at Chawton where Jane lived with her mother, sister Cassandra and family friend Martha Lloyd was painted in 1809, the year the Austen women came to live there.
LEFT Chawton Cottage has become Jane Austen's House Museum.
OPPOSITE TOP The river Stour flows through the grounds of Godmersham Park.
OPPOSITE CENTRE The Topiary Garden includes clipped yew hedges and a central fountain.
OPPOSITE BOTTOM The Wilderness in spring is carpeted with daffodils and *Anemone blanda*.

In her letters, Jane showed clearly how she loved the domesticity of the house and garden – run and peopled by women. They made their own mead, raised chickens and turkeys for the table, and planted peas, potatoes, gooseberries, currants and strawberries. Whenever Cassandra was away at Godmersham, Jane would write with regular, lively updates, as here in May 1811: 'You cannot imagine – it is not in Human Nature to imagine what a nice walk we have round the Orchard . . . I hear today that an Apricot has been detected on one of the Trees.' The flowers at Chawton would have been simple cottage plants such as mallow, hollyhocks, phlox and sweet William. That same summer she also reported to Cassandra, who was at Godmersham, that the garden was gay with pinks, sweet Williams and columbines.

In this happy atmosphere, Jane began writing again – Cassandra protecting her by taking on the household duties and Mrs Austen immersing herself in the Vegetable Garden. She revised *Sense and Sensibility*, and in 1811 it became her first published novel. She revised *Pride and Prejudice* and started work on *Mansfield Park*; in 1813 *Pride and Prejudice* was published.

Edward often spent the summers at Chawton House, together with his huge family of eleven children – including Jane's favourite niece, Fanny. Jane ate meals with the family and walked often in the grounds. When the house was built in the late sixteenth century, the gardens would have been more formal than in Jane's day. By the eighteenth century they had been laid out in the English landscape style, and it is this unadorned parkland that is depicted in paintings of Chawton House and that Jane would have known.

There was a ha-ha, a serpentine carriage drive around the estate and a Wilderness that had survived the English landscape 'improvements'. Just behind the house was a Shrubbery of native trees and shrubs, meant to echo the wild, but with a 'well-drained' gravel path on which ladies and gentleman could walk. In fact, Chawton had every outdoor setting necessary for the characters of *Emma, Mansfield Park* and *Persuasion*, some of the books Jane wrote while living in the village.

Changing Fortunes

Jane's new-found – although still modest – fame and income allowed her to travel to London and to visit Godmersham. She could also

OPPOSITE AND OPPOSITE BELOW Jane knew of her brother Edward's plans to build the new Walled Garden at Chawton House, but did not live to see it.

LEFT The Wilderness dates from the late seventeenth and early eighteenth centuries. It was originally laid out geometrically with trees in straight lines, but this was gradually dropped in favour of more informal paths.

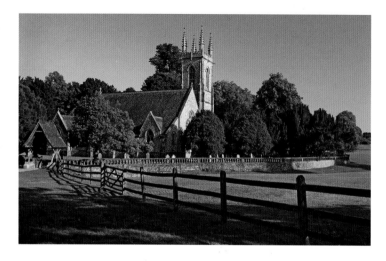

enjoy the occasional luxury of new dress fabrics, or attend a ball. But in 1815 the security of their life at Chawton was threatened by a lawsuit and claim of title for the estate. Edward had to pay £15,000 – a huge sum – and at the same time Henry suffered heavy losses at his bank, in the nearby town of Alton. In comparison, in her entire lifetime, Jane earned only £800 from her writing.

Jane became increasingly ill and died at the premature age of forty-one in 1817. She was buried in Winchester cathedral, near the house in which she had spent her last days, rather than at the little church of St Nicholas beside Chawton House, where Cassandra and Mrs Austen were laid to rest. Cassandra lived on alone at the cottage for almost thirty years without the sister who had been so much part of her being. The church seems a perfect setting for the weddings of two sisters who found happiness in *Pride and Prejudice*, but for the real Austen sisters it was not to be.

One garden feature that Jane had been looking forward to was Edward's longed-for Walled Garden. In July 1813 she had written to her brother Frank: 'Edward . . . talks of making a new Garden; the present one is a bad one and ill situated – he means to have the new at the top of the lawn behind his own house.' In fact, it did not get started until 1818, a year after Jane's death. Ornamental kitchen gardens were the order of the day, and the current garden reflects this bountiful mix of flowers, fruit and vegetables – all grown organically.

Chawton House was handed down to Jane's great-nephew, Montagu Knight, who lived there until 1914. He was responsible for adding the Edwardian terraces – very much in the Arts & Crafts style and possibly designed by his friend Edwin Lutyens.

Restoration Story

Both Chawton Cottage and Chawton House might not have survived without the dedication of an unusual band of people. In 1940 two sisters, Miss Dorothy and Miss Beatrix Darnell, established the Jane Austen Society in order to rescue the cottage in which Jane Austen had spent her happiest last years. Their appeal for funds was not met in total. However, a private individual, Mr T. Edward Carpenter, bought Chawton Cottage and presented it to the nation, setting up the Jane Austen Memorial Trust and opening the cottage as a museum in July 1949.

Chawton House remained – and remains – in the ownership of the Knight family, but by 1987 had fallen into such dereliction that there were fears it would have to be pulled down. The lease was sold to an American entrepreneur and philanthropist, Sandy Lerner, who was an Austenite and collector of early women's writing. She took a 125-year lease and set about restoring the house and gardens – a process that continues today. Along with the Knight family books and Sandy Lerner's own collection, there is now a library of some 11,000 rare books, which forms the basis of the Chawton House Library. This public-access library of women's writings from 1600 to approximately 1830 – much of it accessible online – opened to the public in 2003.

OPPOSITE TOP The Knight family, who owned Chawton House, adopted Jane's brother Edward, and he inherited the estate in 1794. Although Edward and his descendants added features to the gardens, they remain essentially in the English landscape style of the eighteenth century.
OPPOSITE CENTRE Chawton House, including this side door, was built by John Knight between 1583 and the mid-1600s.
OPPOSITE BOTTOM The church of St Nicholas, Chawton sits at the entrance to Chawton House. Jane's mother and sister are buried in the churchyard there.

Written in Residence

STEVENTON AND GODMERSHAM, 1775–1801
Jane Austen began writing 'First Impressions' (later to become *Pride and Prejudice*) in 1796 and returned to 'Elinor and Marianne', a story she had started earlier. Winter 1797 and spring 1798 were spent rewriting 'Elinor and Marianne' – renaming it *Sense and Sensibility*. She then started on the first draft of 'Susan', which would later become *Northanger Abbey*.

CHAWTON, 1809–17
Sense and Sensibility (revised and published 1811)
Pride and Prejudice (revised and published 1813)
Mansfield Park (written 1811–13; published 1814)
Emma (written 1814–15; published 1816)
Northanger Abbey (revised 1816;
published posthumously 1818)
Persuasion (written 1815–16;
published posthumously 1818)
Sanditon (begun 1817; unfinished title on which Jane was working during her last illness; fragment published 1925)

A three-volume first edition of *Pride and Prejudice*

Rupert Brooke at Grantchester

Poet Rupert Brooke will be forever associated with the village of Grantchester, just outside Cambridge. It was here, in 1909, as a graduate of King's College, that he rented rooms, first at Orchard House and then, a year or so later, next door at The Old Vicarage, in order to escape the social whirl of college.

Brooke was charmed and charming – a clearly beautiful, young man, who attracted people to him. His poems, too, shone, although his following grew more fervent after his death during the First World War, at the age of twenty-seven. He seems to represent something that can never be recaptured – the halcyon innocence of pre-war days, which were forever bathed in a golden light. And when, on a trip to Berlin in 1912, Brooke sat in a café and wrote a homesick ode to his life at The Old Vicarage, the place and poet became inseparable in our minds. He lived there for only three years, yet the aura that he left is tangible to this day.

The Old Vicarage, built sometime before 1685, stands on the winding road that leads out of Grantchester towards Trumpington, and its gardens reach down to a millstream. This flows to the river Granta, with its famous water meadows just beyond. The novelist Jeffrey Archer and his wife, Mary, moved there in the late 1970s, and the house's history is told by Dame Mary in her book *The Story of The Old Vicarage Grantchester*.

In 1851 it was bought by a local man, Page Widnall. His father had been a nurseryman growing dahlias in Grantchester, and Page created at The Old Vicarage a garden with flowers and trees and lawns for himself, his wife and sister-in-law. They were keen amateur botanists, and the gardens were the

'Oh! there the chestnuts, summer through,
Beside the river make for you,
A tunnel of green gloom, and sleep
Deeply above; and green and deep
The stream mysterious glides beneath . . .'

'THE OLD VICARAGE, GRANTCHESTER'

setting of many happy Victorian gatherings. Page was responsible for building the 'castle ruin' (a Gothic-style folly made from soft limestone and clay, where he set up a printing press), a summer house and a 'Swiss cottage' – all the rage at the time. He wrote a history of Grantchester and invented a 'folding form' (backrests to be used when sitting out in the gardens), which he patented.

The romantic ruin (Brooke's 'The falling house that never falls'), the fast-flowing millstream and the old horse chestnuts at the bottom of the garden captured the hearts of everyone who visited the house. And so it was for Brooke who, having left the city, wrote to Noël Olivier about his life by the river: 'You know the place; it is near all picnicking grounds. And here I work at Shakespeare and see few people. In the intervals I wander about bare foot and almost naked, surveying Nature. I do not

LEFT While studying at Cambridge, poet Rupert Brooke (1887–1915) took lodgings by the river at Grantchester.
RIGHT The river Granta runs below the gardens of The Old Vicarage, Granchester.

pretend to understand Nature, but I get on very well with her . . .
I go on with my books, and she goes on with her hens and storms
and things, and we're both very tolerant. I live on honey, eggs and
milk . . . and sit all day in a rose garden to work.'

It was not true that Brooke saw few people. His friendships and
love affairs were complex and fed his poetic life. Virginia Woolf swam
with him in the river, E.M. Forster, Maynard Keynes, Augustus John
and the philosophers Bertrand Russell and Ludwig Wittgenstein, as
well as Brooke's girlfriends Noël Olivier and Ka Cox, all gathered at
The Old Vicarage and sat either in The Orchard or in the Vicarage
gardens. When Keynes visited in 1909 he found Brooke surrounded
by women and wearing nothing but a sweater. Duncan Grant
painted Brooke's girlfriend in the summer house there in 1911 (and
put up an impromptu display of his pictures). Brooke's landlord,
Henry Neeve, was a beekeeper, so there probably was, as the last
line of his most famous poem says, always honey for tea.

Brooke wrote poetry prolifically while at Grantchester, sitting
out on the lawn by the veranda. His first collection (and the only
one published while he was alive) contained poems from 1905 to
1911 – the Cambridge and Grantchester years. These poems are
filled with the joy of being alive, of being young and in love, yet
have that tinge of sadness and recognition of mortality that were
to be prophetic.

OPPOSITE ABOVE LEFT The Old Vicarage has been home to Jeffrey and Mary Archer since 1979.

OPPOSITE ABOVE RIGHT Rupert Brooke often studied and wrote in the garden. Here, in 1911, he is busy translating plays from Swedish into English for Miss Estrid Linden, who also took the photograph.

OPPOSITE BELOW A path to a thatched summer house leads past a magnolia and borders filled with blue forget-me-nots.

LEFT The Folly, which Brooke referred to as the 'falling house that never falls', was rebuilt by the Archers.

The Orchard

The apple and cherry trees at Orchard House, next to The Old Vicarage, were planted in 1868. In 1897 a group of Cambridge students asked the landlady, Mrs Stevenson, if they could take tea beneath the blossom (rather than by the house), and a tradition was born. Mrs Stevenson and her daughters served tea from a tin-roofed hut, and it soon became a popular destination for students, as it still is today. They arrive on foot across the Grantchester Meadows, by bicycle or by canoe or punt up the river Granta. Among those it has welcomed are academics, politicians, writers, actors, artists and occasional royalty. A.E. Housman, A.A. Milne, Sylvia Plath and John Betjeman have all sat beneath the trees and imagined themselves to be in Arcadia.

In 1987 this place of great literary pilgrimage nearly disappeared when the land on which The Orchard stands was earmarked for housing development. It was rescued by Robin Callan, who bought it in 1992 and reinstated it for its original purpose. There is a small Rupert Brooke Museum – run by the Rupert Brooke Society – and there is, of course, 'honey still for tea' . . . even if it is now inevitably served in little pots rather than from straight from the comb.

BELOW LEFT and BELOW RIGHT Cherry (below left) and apple blossom (below right) still bloom each spring in The Orchard, which has been a place of literary pilgrimage for more than a century.

However, it was the later volume, published after his death in 1915, that ensured Brooke's poetic immortality. It contained his '1914 War Sonnets' and his 1912 poem, 'The Old Vicarage, Grantchester' – at first entitled simply 'Home'. He was thirsting for the quiet of Grantchester and particularly The Old Vicarage, which he had come to call home. He observed and absorbed the garden on a deep level and felt that it was 'his' when he wrote:

Just now the lilac is in bloom
All before my little room;
And in my flower-beds, I think,
Smile the carnation and the pink;
And down the borders, well I know,
The poppy and the pansy blow . . .

In Literary Footsteps

It would be strange if this past did not spill over into the present. Indeed, the current owner, Jeffrey Archer, has used the upper part of Page Widnall's 'castle ruin' – renamed The Folly – as his writing room for the past thirty-five years. His first novel, *Not A Penny More, Not A Penny Less*, was published in 1975, and his family moved to Grantchester in 1979, when Mary took up an academic post at the University of Cambridge Department of Chemistry.

The Archers are avid art collectors, and set into the walls of The Folly are two stone reliefs by the great sculptor and letter-cutter Eric Gill. They restored The Folly in 1990 to make it more habitable and less damp. The gardens too have been developed, with ponds, herbaceous borders, lawns and areas of meadow and woodland, where visitors encounter quirky, sculpted hares and geese by contemporary artists.

ABOVE LEFT Horse chestnut trees overhang the millstream at the bottom of The Old Vicarage garden.
ABOVE RIGHT 'Stands the church clock at ten to three? And is there honey still for tea?' It is not known if Brooke wrote these lines because the clock really had stopped at this time, but it has come to symbolize the way time stood still for Brooke – who never returned to Grantchester.

Dame Mary and her gardener have planted and reshaped the garden to suit its twenty-first-century use as a family garden. They have scooped out a natural hollow to create a large pond (known as Lake Oscar, after a family cat) and put up a wooden bridge across it. This is now festooned with wisteria. Borders have been extended and replanted with herbaceous planting and flowering shrubs and trees – hornbeams, maple, willow and oak. The family particularly monitors the horse chestnuts that line the riverside as they are elderly and suffering from disease. These are the trees that Brooke remembered in his poem and that his friend Gwen Darwin (later Raverat) captured in her woodcut of 1937.

Yet at The Old Vicarage there is just enough wilderness to remind one of the pre-First-World-War idyll that stole Rupert Brooke's heart. Down by the water, cow parsley and wild flowers flourish, and on a little island in the millstream a pair of swans make their nest year after year. A century on, Brooke is somehow still casting his spell over Grantchester.

ABOVE LEFT, ABOVE CENTRE AND ABOVE RIGHT Lilac (above left) was one of Brooke's favourite flowers, while cow parsley, alkanet (above centre) and red campion (above right) grow in the meadow.

RIGHT TOP The footbridge at Grantchester is festooned with wisteria in late spring.

RIGHT CENTRE The display reliefs in the arcades of the Folly were created by the great sculptor Eric Gill.

RIGHT BOTTOM The Guardian Hare sculpture in the wild, wooded area near the millstream is by Stanley Dove.

Written in Residence

RUPERT BROOKE, 1909–12

Brooke's first book of fifty poems (and the only volume issued during his lifetime) was published in 1911. It contained poems written at Grantchester, which reflected the loves, losses and emotional turmoils of a young man and included: 'Dust' (1909–10), 'The Hill' (1910), and 'Kindliness' (1910).

His best-loved poems are those he wrote when looking back at his idyllic life at Grantchester: 'The Old Vicarage, Grantchester' (1912); and his eerily prophetic *1914 Sonnets (I–V)*, which include the lines:

> *'If I should die, think only this of me:*
> *That there's some corner of a foreign field*
> *That is for ever England.'*
> 'V. The Soldier'

Brooke died aboard a hospital ship on 23 April 1915 from blood poisoning. He was, as the poem prophesied, buried by his comrades in a 'foreign field' – in an olive grove on the nearby Greek island of Skyros.

JEFFREY ARCHER, 1979–

Jeffrey Archer took up residence at The Old Vicarage in 1979, when his third novel – *Kane and Abel* – was about to be published. The advance came just in time to put a down payment on the house with its garden ruin, which he intended to use as a writing room. Lord Archer went on to write another seventeen novels (including *The Prodigal Daughter* 1982, *Honour Among Thieves* 1993 and *The Best Kept Secret* 2013) as well as his prison diaries, short stories and plays. Lord Archer continues to write and has sold more than 270 million books worldwide.

John Ruskin at Brantwood

In spring, the lanes to Brantwood on the eastern shore of Coniston Water wind through verges of wild garlic, fern-studded slate walls, and woods full of bluebells. These are the lanes that John Ruskin first visited as a boy of five and again at eighteen, when he rowed his boat into Brantwood harbour and sat in a field, sketching Coniston Hall across the lake, directly below the house that thirty years later would become his home.

The scent of the wild garlic soon gives way to the garden's giddy colour and the heady scent of yellow azaleas (*Rhododendron luteum*). Welsh poppies (*Meconopsis cambrica*), yellow tree peonies, fresh fronds of ferns, wild strawberries, saxifrage and epimediums cover the ground, with touches of blue from aquilegias. This is an artist's garden – even though Ruskin was much more than an artist.

Ruskin had grown up in Herne Hill in south London and, with parents who filled his mind with religion, art and poetry, was destined to become something special. Born in 1819 – the same year as Queen Victoria – and also living to see out the nineteenth century, he was a true Victorian. Yet, he was not at all typical of the time. He was a great draughtsman and watercolourist (idolizing Turner), but became best known as an art critic. He came from a family in trade, but began to question the wealth and human cost of the Industrial Revolution. He was raised in suburban gentility, but became one of the most outspoken radical conservationists Britain had known. He raised issues about pollution, poverty and climate change, which still resonate in the twenty-first century.

In 1871, at the age of fifty-two, Ruskin was at the height of his success as a writer, academic (he had recently become the first Slade Professor of Art at Oxford), speaker and artist. He had completed his epic, five-volume *Modern Painters* (started when he was only twenty-four), and his book *Stones of Venice* had catapulted him to fame. He was undertaking gruelling lecture tours as well as keeping up his non-stop writing of pamphlets, on everything from Greek birds to Tuscan art. Yet his inner life was in turmoil. His short marriage to Euphemia ('Effie') Gray had been annulled in 1854 on the grounds

'It's a bit of steep hillside, facing west . . . the slope is half copse, half moor and rock – a pretty field beneath.'

JOHN RUSKIN, 1871

The gardens at Brantwood slope down to the shores of Coniston Water in Cumbria.

THE WRITER'S GARDEN

THE WRITER'S GARDEN

of non-consummation, and his relationship with Rose la Touche (whom he had proposed to when she was just eighteen) was in its final throes. He was hounded for his outspoken theories; dubbed a radical, he was both celebrated and shot down.

Ruskin was ill and looking for respite. He yearned for the lakes and Coniston Water in particular, which represented all his youthful ideals – of landscape painting, romantic poetry and peace.

He bought Brantwood, unseen, for £1,500 and, when he arrived, found the view was even better than he remembered. He set to work straight away, and in September 1871 reported working all day clearing the garden and watching the weeds being burnt in the twilight. He moved there in September 1872, with his young cousin Joan Severn and her artist husband Arthur, who came up frequently from London to look after his domestic life. The house itself was described as small, old and damp – a two-storey cottage, with a bank of turf in front of it, which was improved and extended over the years.

From the first, Ruskin threw his considerable mental and physical energies into the estate, revelling in the manual labour. He enlarged the harbour and built terraces, bridges over streams, paths and steps up and down the rocky hillside. He installed reservoirs, and commissioned a rowing boat called *Jumping Jenny*.

The garden provided Ruskin with an outdoor laboratory for his intensive studies of nature and man. An early project was to make a small, productive, experimental garden, mixing fruit, flowers and herbs in an informal way. This garden just above the house became known as The Professor's Garden, and here he grew gooseberry bushes, strawberries and flowers and built a beehive shelter. Next came the Zig-Zaggy, a convoluted path climbing up the hillside, where he put into practice his ideas on cultivating steep ground. This offered an allegorical approach, climbing the purgatorial mount to paradise – inspired by Dante's *Divine Comedy*. The Zig-Zaggy includes the sheep's wool 'knot', made in dark wool from local Herdwick sheep and white wool from other breeds, which is renewed each spring. Lower down, near the lake, there were kitchen gardens.

Everything at Brantwood was multifunctional, designed not only to be practical and fun but also experimental, scientific and often

Written in Residence

BRANTWOOD, 1872–1900

John Ruskin spent the last three decades of his life at Brantwood, using the gardens as a laboratory for his thinking and writing.

Mornings in Florence (1875–7)

Fiction, Fair and Foul (1880–81)

The Bible of Amiens (1880–85)

The Storm Cloud of the Nineteenth Century (1884)

Praeterita (1885–9) – meaning, Of Past Things, Autobiography

John Ruskin (1819–1900) at Brantwood

allegorical or spiritual. Ruskin saw nature intensely, and leaned always towards the natural in his choice of plants.

Ruskin's cousin Joan – who often seems to have had the upper hand in the garden – planted rhododendrons, azaleas and many other fashionable plants. She wanted greenhouses to grow tender plants, but Ruskin was against them; however, he eventually capitulated. He favoured simple flowers, writing in 1877: 'I believe no manner or temperance in pleasure would be better rewarded than that of making our gardens gay only with common flowers.'

Ruskin was a new kind of gardener, working with the natural lie of the land and adding wild and indigenous species. His leaning towards the wild was not a lone voice. William Robinson's book *The Wild Garden* had come out in 1870, and Ruskin had both corresponded with and contributed to journals published by him.

He studied how everything grew very carefully, not only with his artist's eye but also with his mind – as a social and environmental reformer. Ruskin believed gardening was good for people: 'No words, no thoughts can measure the possible change for good which energetic and tender care of the wild herbs of the fields and trees of the wood might bring . . . to the bodily pleasure and the mental power of man.' He was interested in how marginal land could be brought into cultivation to alleviate poverty while still respecting its natural character and ecology. Following this principle of serving man while caring for nature, he developed a Moorland Garden higher up the hillside, draining the ground and creating two new reservoirs.

Visions of the Future

Ruskin's years at Brantwood – his twilight years – were not entirely happy, although they were productive. He got up early and worked from his study on the ground floor, overlooking the lake. In his lifetime it was estimated that he wrote nine million words. He suffered bouts of mental illness, and had such bad nightmares or hallucinations that he would no longer sleep in his own bedroom, where he had built a 'turret' looking out over the countryside. Yet he was a man who touched and continues to touch many people's lives.

As he withdrew to his lakeside retreat at Brantwood, others would take up the causes Ruskin had first championed. He had challenged the 'rightness' of industrial progress that ripped people away from

LEFT In Ruskin's time, the area nearest the water was used as a Kitchen Garden. Now, it is the Harbour Walk and is lined with bright azaleas and rhododendrons.
BELOW LEFT Stone steps lead to The Professor's Garden.
BELOW Ruskin favoured natural materials and native plants.

ABOVE LEFT Old tree stumps make a natural setting for Welsh poppies and ferns on the steep slope of the Zig-Zaggy.

ABOVE RIGHT Native ferns have been planted at the foot of the mature maple (*Acer*) trees, along the path leading up to the High Walk.

the countryside and their roots. He was an early environmentalist, and was the first to suggest that we should 'conserve' buildings – not restore them. He pointed out that buildings belonged to the people who built them and to the people who would come after them – the current generation were simply custodians and should not do anything to the buildings that could not be reversed. At Brantwood he acted out his beliefs – the right, for example, of every person to lead an intellectual as well as a practical, physical life.

When he was well enough, Ruskin encouraged visitors, including Charles Darwin, who came to dinner on several occasions. His influence was felt worldwide: Tolstoy said of him that he was one of those rare men who thought with their hearts.

Ruskin died in January 1900 and was buried, as he had wanted, in Coniston churchyard, overlooking Brantwood. Through his sometimes tortured life he had watched the natural world and concluded that, in the end, 'There is no wealth but life.'

The Gardens in the Twenty-first Century

The 8.5 hectares / 20 acres of garden (within the wider 101-hectare / 250-acre estate) is being managed to take up the challenge where Ruskin left off. In his day, there was a lot of help – up to twenty-two gardeners and estate workers were employed to help realize his vision.

The current team is necessarily very much smaller, but the principles of a landscape in which social, environmental and aesthetic principles are considered as a whole is still the goal. When renovation began in the 1980s, the garden had become very overgrown, and it was only through a combination of research and garden archaeology that the team uncovered its history. Little by little, the discovery of Ruskin's garden projects proved that this was his laboratory of thinking – the place where he had put his principles into practice and explored what was on his mind. He had been fascinated by what the land could do and had carried out experiments into the effects of water and wind weathering.

The historic garden structures – the walls and paths – are now restored, and there have been new additions such as the Fern Garden planted with British native ferns. This was both a homage to William James Linton, who lived at Brantwood before Ruskin and published the first Lakeland-fern flora, and to Ruskin himself, who studied native plants.

There are longer-term goals: to extend the Moorland Garden; and to continue Ruskin's experiment of learning to communicate the need to reconnect fully with nature. Already, the field where Ruskin first sketched is the subject of a biodynamic land experiment. The challenge is to make his research relevant to the twenty-first century – to 'unpack' his ideas for a new generation.

Literary Connections

Before John Ruskin, Brantwood was the home of William James Linton, an artist, poet and political writer and leading wood-engraver of his day. He set up his own printing press in the outbuildings, and his second wife, Eliza Lynn Linton, was a popular novelist, writing *Lizzie Lorton of Greyrigg* and *Grasp Your Nettle* while at Brantwood. Linton rented a garden and two fields between the house and lake and went on to publish *The Ferns of the English Lake Country* (1865).

Golden male fern (*Dryopteris affinis*)

Agatha Christie at Greenway

Greenway is a garden to get lost in. When walking the woodland paths as the sun disappears and the last visitors leave, there is a distinct chill in the air. A breeze slides up the river Dart, and even the voices of the day trippers on the boats and paddle steamers seem to recede. The walls of the now-demolished glasshouses in the Camellia Garden make it dark and dank. You would be forgiven for turning round to look over your shoulder to see if you are quite alone . . . well this is Agatha Christie's garden, and the Stable Yard clock does strike at a few minutes past the hour.

Greenway was not Agatha's first nor only garden, but it is the one that has become most strongly identified with the woman who became the world's bestselling crime writer. Her childhood was spent at Ashfield, a large Victorian villa in Torquay, where she

was born in 1890, the treasured youngest child of three. She was tutored at home, allowed to roam the Kitchen Garden and played croquet and tennis on the lawns. Soon Agatha Miller (as she was at the time) began to explore the darker boundaries of her safe world: '. . . there was the wood. In my imagination it loomed as large as the New Forest . . . The wood had everything . . . mystery, terror, secret delight, inaccessibility and distance. When you emerged, enchantment ended. You were in the everyday world once more.'

Ashfield remained in the Miller family through the deaths of her parents, and through Agatha's stormy first marriage to Archibald Christie and the birth of her daughter, Rosalind. In fact, so attached was she to the memories stored at Ashfield that she could not bear to part with it until she was fifty years old. By then she was happily married to her second husband, the archaeologist Max Mallowan, and living at Winterbrook House, Wallingford. It was convenient for the University at Oxford and had a long garden going down to the Thames. Yet Agatha always called it 'Max's House' and retained a hopeless infatuation with Devon. In her heart nothing could replace Ashfield . . . until, in 1938, she got the chance to buy Greenway and its 14.5 hectares / 36 acres for £6,000. By then she was an extremely successful novelist.

Agatha could not believe that such a place could be hers. and she somehow always feared it was too good to be true. In fact, her fears were well founded – Greenway was requisitioned for war use by the US Coast Guard in October 1942. Agatha was not able to see it again until Christmas 1945: 'Greenway was beautiful when we went down there again on a sunny winter's day – but it was wild. Wild as a beautiful jungle. Paths had disappeared, the Kitchen Garden . . . was all a mass of weeds and the fruit trees had not been pruned. It was sad in many ways . . . but its beauty was still there.'

Greenway before Agatha Christie

From a gardener's perspective, Greenway has a fascinating history before being bought by Agatha Christie. It stands on a promontory

'They went on, down a steep hill through woods, then through big iron gates, and along a drive, winding up finally in front of a big white Georgian house.'

DEAD MAN'S FOLLY

OPPOSITE AND LEFT Agatha Christie fell head over heels in love with Greenway, the white Georgian house standing in wooded grounds above the estuary of the river Dart, in Devon.

THE WRITER'S GARDEN

above a bend in the river Dart, just upstream from the naval port of Dartmouth. During the Spanish Armada, Sir Francis Drake captured a Spanish vessel, and while their ship was held in Dartmouth the crew were put to work building the walls and paths of Greenway for Sir John Gilbert – half-brother to Sir Walter Raleigh.

There was a house on the site – known as Greenway Court – from the sixteenth century, but the current house is Georgian, being built around 1780. It was bought by Bristol merchant Edward Elton in the 1790s, and it was he who made the Camellia Garden and the entrance drive. However, it was the Carlyon family who would have the most horticultural influence on Greenway, buying in Turkey oaks and the tulip tree (*Liriodendron tulipifera*), which stands near the house. In 1841 Edward Carlyon inherited Tregrehan in Cornwall, and so he moved there – with, it is thought, many of the plants from Greenway. The Cornish connection continued with Richard Harvey, who bought the house in 1852 and whose cousin was restoring Caerhays Castle; he added the glasshouses to the Walled Garden and introduced exotics such as acacias, clianthus, sophoras and myrtles.

The £6,000 Agatha paid for Greenway can be put in context by the fact that, in 1882, Thomas Bolitho bought the estate for £44,000 (albeit at that time it was much larger, being 121 hectares/300 acres or so). During his time, there were records of phormiums, callistemons, abutilons and Banksian roses being grown. His daughter took over the running of the estate with her husband, Charles Williams of Caerhays, who was a knowledgeable and keen plantsman. Narcissi, rhododendrons and especially magnolias were ordered from Cornish nurseries, and Greenway became, almost, the garden we see today – a fascinating mix of the exotic, the rare, the wild and the commonplace.

The Mallowans

When at Greenway, Agatha and Max were known simply as 'the Mallowans'. Agatha craved privacy after the affair of her first husband, and her subsequent 'disappearance' had left her bruised and fearful of the press and too much public attention. They loved the shelter that the mature trees and shrubs gave them from the passing river boats and day trippers on the estuary.

One of the first things they did was to ask Williams to return to identify the shrubs and trees. Neither of them was particularly knowledgeable, but they wanted to learn and do their best for the garden. By 1949 they had set up a nursery in the old Kitchen Garden. Also in 1949, Agatha's daughter, Rosalind, whose first husband had been killed in the Second World War, married Anthony Hicks. As Agatha's fame grew through the 1950s with the new media of film and television, the Hickses took on the running of Greenway.

Nearest the house, magnolias predominate. The west lawn has an old *Magnolia grandiflora*, and down the slope there are specimen *M. denudata* and *M. × veitchii*. Overhanging the stable yard – which is now where afternoon tea is served – there are several old *M. campbellii*, which scatter their soft pink petals over the cobblestones.

Agatha was passionate about Greenway and often felt guilty that she could not care for it properly while she was away with husband Max on his digs in Iraq. (Max was the force behind the digging of Nimrud – a site that had not been investigated for a hundred years. Agatha wrote *4.50 from Paddington* while out in Nimrud.)

ABOVE Greenway sits on a promontory above the river Dart in Devon. LEFT Sir Francis Drake spent time on the river Dart estuary during the Spanish Armada, and Greenway was once owned by a half-brother to Sir Walter Raleigh.

Yet when they were at Greenway, it was filled with love and laughter – Rosalind, Anthony, Agatha's grandson Mathew Prichard and numerous other members of the family as well as friends used the gardens, playing tennis and messing about in boats on the river. According to Mathew, Greenway was at the centre of the family's life after the Second World War: 'We spent the summers there; slowly the hardships and sacrifices of the war disappeared. My grandmother went there every year having completed a book, so a sense of wellbeing engulfed us . . . The beautiful garden, replete with peaches and nectarines, rhododendrons and camellias, entered its halcyon days.'

Agatha spent her last Christmas at Greenway in 1973. A few years earlier, she looked back over her life and the houses she had lived in. 'When I dream, I hardly ever dream of Greenway, or Winterbrook', she wrote. 'It is always Ashfield.' And when it was pulled down in the early 1960s, she wept bitterly.

A New Era

Perhaps Greenway did not need her tears; it was a beloved house and one that went on after she had gone. Max, Rosalind and Anthony lived on there for the rest of their lives. A new era in Greenway's history began in 2000, when it was given to the National Trust, although the family have continued to be involved in its care.

The beauty of Greenway is that, even with the substantial numbers of visitors it attracts, the crowds dissipate as soon as you wander even a little way from the house. It is a garden of light and shade – of bright sunlit lawns and winding woodland paths through, in spring, plantings of primroses, wild garlic and bluebells. The paths, which were once hard, worn, muddy tracks, have now, inevitably, been widened and hard-cored to suit Greenway's transition from family home to public garden.

The shelter belt of trees planted during the eighteenth and nineteenth centuries includes countless rhododendrons, magnolias and camellias, as well as many unusual species of oak, pine, chestnut and beech. Agatha enjoyed the privacy these trees gave and encouraged more planting: she and Max planted thickly – for today, not for tomorrow.

The National Trust team has now spent a decade assessing and cataloguing the plants (3,000 recorded so far) and is still discovering introductions from the southern hemisphere, including Chile and Australia. These are now being given room to grow, and at the same time the gardeners are thinning and opening up the vistas again, to give glimpses of the banks of the Dart.

The woodland paths at Greenway twist and turn, but finally lead to the edge of the promontory and the Battery – a Napoleonic defence that features in several Agatha Christie novels. She described it almost exactly in *Five Little Pigs*: 'For a moment Poirot was dazzled coming in from the shade outside. The Battery was an artificially cleared plateau with battlements set with cannon. It gave one the impression of overhanging the sea. There were trees above it and behind it, but on the sea side there was nothing but the dazzling blue water below.'

A path also winds down to the boathouse – known as Raleigh's Boathouse – although in fact it is a later construction. Farther down the slope is the Camellia Garden, which includes the remains of

ABOVE Agatha and her husband, the archaeologist Max Mallowan, relax on the Battery at Greenway in 1946.
RIGHT The Battery dates from the Napoleonic wars. It became the setting for several scenes in Agatha Christie's novels, including the poisoning of an artist in *Five Little Pigs*.

hothouses perhaps once used to protect camellias. Actually, these plants thrive without protection in the mild Devon climate.

There are two walled gardens at Greenway. The South Walled Garden was the original Kitchen Garden. It contains an old *Wisteria sinensis*, the remnants of some old espalier apples and a Vinery against the south wall; otherwise, the South Walled Garden is a lawned space used for theatre productions and events. The North Walled Garden now houses the working areas and the restored Peach House. This was where the Hickses ran a commercial nursery, and there are plans to produce more plants on site.

In the twenty-first century, Greenway has entered a new phase, as Agatha and her family take their place among the pantheon of plant collectors, naval heroes and adventurers who made it what it is.

ABOVE LEFT, ABOVE CENTRE AND ABOVE RIGHT A survey of many of the rhododendrons at Greenway is ongoing, and this deep red variety has yet to be finally identified (above left); *Rhododendron* 'Boddaertianum' (above centre); *Magnolia* x *soulangeana* (above right).
RIGHT TOP Bluebells carpet the slopes of Greenway in spring.
RIGHT CENTRE In the Boathouse, a body is found in *Dead Man's Folly*.
RIGHT BOTTOM The Bird Pond has a sculpture by Bridget McCrum.

Written in Residence

GREENWAY, 1938–76

Famously, Agatha Christie claimed she could write anywhere, as long as she had a steady table and a typewriter. From *The Mysterious Affair at Styles* (1920) – introducing the Belgian detective Hercule Poirot – to her last full-length Marple case, *Sleeping Murder* (1976), she wrote more than a hundred novels, plays, short stories and non-fiction books.

THE GREENWAY NOVELS
Five Little Pigs (1943)
Dead Man's Folly (1956)
Ordeal by Innocence (1958)

A SELECTION OF OTHER WORKS
A Murder is Announced (Marple) (1950)
4.50 from Paddington (Marple) (1957)
The Mirror Crack'd from Side to Side (1962)
Curtain: Poirot's Last Case (1975)

Agatha Christie (1890–1976) at Greenway

THE WRITER'S GARDEN

Beatrix Potter at Hill Top

To anyone who has enjoyed a Beatrix Potter book as a child or read them to their own children or grandchildren, Hill Top in the village of Near Sawrey will already seem familiar. The slate-topped farmhouse with its porches, paths and cottage borders, and the Vegetable Garden with its green-painted gate, are just as they were when Beatrix used them as the backdrop to the adventures of Jemima Puddle-duck, Tom Kitten and Samuel Whiskers.

In 1905, at the age of thirty-nine, the already successful children's author and artist bought a collection of buildings and land known as Hill Top Farm in the southern part of the Lake District. She had already written the first stories about Peter Rabbit, Squirrel Nutkin, Benjamin Bunny and Mrs Tiggy-winkle while living with her parents in London. Beatrix had also recently lost her fiancé, the publisher Norman Warne, who had not only cherished her talent but also loved her as a person. She was bereft and in need of something to take her away from the stifling expectations of her parents and London middle-class life.

With the money from her books and a legacy from a relative, Beatrix paid £2,805 for Hill Top Farm and its 14 hectares / 34 acres – almost double the price it had previously changed hands for. She did not care. The Potters had been coming to the Lake District for years, often staying at Wray Castle a few kilometres from Near Sawrey, and now she would own her own patch of the landscape she had fallen in love with.

Although it would only ever be a part-time home, Hill Top gave Beatrix the chance to put into practice all the aesthetic and practical ideas she had stored up over the years about houses and gardens. She was influenced by the Arts & Crafts movement, by things she had seen and done in her travels, and possibly by the great gardener of the time Gertrude Jekyll. She set about extending the house, adding a wing for the tenant farmer who would continue to live there and farm the land. She rendered the outside of the building with grey pebbledash, to disguise the new additions – she had a horror

'There is a quarryman who lives on the road to the ferry who has got some most splendid phloxes, they will look nice between the laurels . . . I shall plant the lilies between the azaleas . . .'

BEATRIX POTTER, 1906

The Vegetable Garden at Hill Top Farm in the Lake District is a glorious mix of edible and ornamental plants.

OPPOSITE, OPPOSITE CENTRE AND OPPOSITE RIGHT *Paeonia officinalis* (opposite) white saxifrage (opposite centre) and *Iris sibirica* (opposite right) are all plants that Beatrix grew in the garden of Hill Top.
BELOW The blooms of *Wisteria floribunda* 'Alba' adorn the front porch at Hill Top in late spring and early summer.
BELOW RIGHT The path through the cottage borders is made from local Lakeland slate.

of whitewashed houses, which she felt stood out too much in the landscape. She also furnished the interior with old oak furniture and carefully chosen pieces, creating her own romantic, idealized version of a Lakeland country farmhouse.

Now, for the first time, Beatrix had her own outside space, which would become her solace and her inspiration. She tackled the gardens with a vengeance, again playing out all the ideas she had stored in her mind, particularly from her aunt and uncle's Walled Garden at

THE WRITER'S GARDEN

Gwaynynog in Wales, which featured in *The Tale of the Flopsy Bunnies*. She moved the driveway, making more room for a garden in front of the house, adding wicket gates on the roadside, which then, as now, offered two routes in – one to the farm and one to the house. She built new walls, and the existing Kitchen Garden was joined by a new paddock and flower beds bordering a pathway of Brathay stone slabs.

Because Beatrix was at Hill Top for only short periods at first, she relied on local workers and so her changes did not always go according to plan. She came back in April 1906 to find that the small lawn and cottage borders she had hoped for had become a huge flat area of grass. She soon rearranged the beds as she wanted them, to create the long cottage borders we see today.

Beatrix acquired plants whenever she could, shamelessly taking them from other people's gardens. Local people would dig up clumps and bring them to her, knowing she had big empty spaces to fill: 'I have been planting hard all day – thanks to a well meant but slightly ill-timed present of saxifrage from Mrs Taylor at the corner cottage,' she wrote to Millie Warne in September 1906.

A Labour of Love

It is rare to find a garden about which we know so much in terms of the original planting. From Beatrix's letters and notes we know she put in azaleas and laurels for shrub cover and interspersed them with lilies, hollyhocks, phlox, saxifrage and Japanese anemones. We learn that the saxifrage was 'longer in the stalk' than the London variety, and, from the photographs taken by her father Rupert, that there were long-stemmed *Primula japonica* among the saxifrage. Beatrix wrote about planting apples, pears and plums in the orchard, and underplanting them with snowdrops and wild daffodils.

The garden was in the cottage style, which was being advocated by Jekyll, and perfectly suited the house. It became, season by season, a labour of love, and Beatrix learned as she went along. She particularly loved the Vegetable Garden, which was surely created with Mr McGregor in mind – she had already written *The Tale of Peter Rabbit*. In terms of materials she was following the Arts & Crafts philosophy of using quality, local materials such as oak, slate and Lakeland stone. She put up an oak trellis along the path, to

Written in Residence

**HILL TOP, 1905–43, AND
CASTLE COTTAGE, 1913–43 (A SELECTION)**

Beatrix Potter moved to Castle Cottage when she
married William Heelis, but used Hill Top for work.

The Tale of Mr Jeremy Fisher (1906)

The Tale of Tom Kitten (1907)

The Tale of Jemima Puddle-duck (1908)

The Roly-poly Pudding (1908), later became

The Tale of Samuel Whiskers

The Tale of Johnny Town-mouse (1918)

Beatrix Potter (1866–1943), outside Hill Top, in summer 1913

the space and support espalier apples – an idea shown in an early sketch she had made of her aunt's garden and which is also clearly depicted in the frontispiece for *The Tale of Tom Kitten*.

What Hill Top did for Beatrix was to release a creative force, which had only just emerged. The interior and exterior were soon being depicted in the books that she wrote from 1905 onwards. Jemima Puddle-duck can be seen in the Vegetable Garden – very much as it is today – and *The Tale of Samuel Whiskers* seems to take place very firmly within the walls and old oak panelling of the house.

A Tale of Two Gardens

In 1913 Beatrix married local solicitor William Heelis and started a new life, moving into Castle Cottage, just on the other side of Near Sawrey. She had already bought several farms in the area (including Castle Farm) and she began to develop two very different personas. One was Mrs Heelis, the farmer and countrywoman, who became progressively involved in local politics and conservation. The other persona was Beatrix Potter, the popular children's author and artist.

At Castle Cottage, Beatrix planted many of her 'old favourites': rhododendrons, azaleas and chaenomeles, with box hedging surrounding cottage plants and roses. Here, she had more space to become a 'real' farmer – the farm buildings were for her use – whereas the ones at Hill Top had always been occupied. There are also glimpses that she was allowing the more cultivated Beatrix to emerge. She built a spacious extension in 1923 and added decorative features that would have had no place at Hill Top, including clipped topiary and decorative (rather than functional) stone walls. From her sitting room in the new extension, Beatrix could look over Hill Top – just as, from the writing room at Hill Top, she could see Castle Cottage.

The two gardens represent different sides of the woman. When she wanted to be 'Miss Potter' she went to Hill Top, where she still wrote and received visitors connected with her work. At Castle Cottage, she was always known as Mrs Heelis the farmer and solicitor's wife, who protected her privacy fiercely.

Castle Cottage was featured in some of her later books, including *The Tale of Johnny Town-mouse*, which is thought to be the most autobiographical of all her 'Tales'. In it, she talks about how different

ABOVE Beatrix Potter had Mr McGregor very much in mind when she created the Vegetable Garden at Hill Top.

LEFT Flowers and perennial vegetables are allowed to jostle for space in the garden.

FOLLOWING PAGES In the village of Near Sawrey, Beatrix divided her time between Hill Top Farm (left) and Castle Cottage (far right).

RIGHT Beatrix Potter lived at Castle
Cottage after her marriage to
William Heelis. The rhododendrons
and azaleas there echo the ones
at Hill Top.

BELOW RIGHT Castle Cottage is on the
edge of the village of Near Sawrey,
and Beatrix could see Hill Top from
its windows.

OPPOSITE TOP In late spring, Hill
Top bursts into bloom after a hard
Lakeland winter.

OPPOSITE CENTRE The old apple
orchard is grazed in the traditional
way, by sheep and lambs.

OPPOSITE BOTTOM White lilac,
pink azaleas and hardy geraniums
surround the walled Vegetable
Garden at Hill Top.

THE WRITER'S GARDEN

places suit different people, but it could equally have applied to the two sides of her personality. When she wanted to be 'Miss Potter' again she could walk down across the lane, through Post Office field and reach one of the little wicket gates in the walls of Hill Top.

A Writer's Legacy

Beatrix and William lived on in Near Sawrey until her death in December 1943; William died a couple of years later. Beatrix left an enormous legacy of land, farms and buildings – some 1,620 hectares / 4,000 acres – which were bequeathed to the National Trust. Thus, this special landscape lives on, as she had intended it.

The garden at Hill Top now recreates the golden years when Beatrix lived there. As far as possible, all the plants in the garden today are ones that we know she grew: cottage plants such as aquilegias, *Iris sibirica*, thalictrum, hardy geraniums, violas, brunnera, lilacs and alchemilla. Fruit and vegetables have strayed from the Kitchen Garden, and lettuces, pumpkins and currants turn up in the flower borders. It is a balance between order and chaos – weeds are allowed, and patches of grass are not strimmed to neatness.

After a hard Lakeland winter, the long borders at Hill Top appear empty – as Beatrix must have experienced them many times since she first made the garden. At that point, it seems nothing will ever grow again. But it does – the plants keeping pace with the weather and catching up so that they all begin to flower at once. The white wisteria on the house breaks into flower before the chaenomeles has finished. Peonies burst open almost before the narcissi have died away. This is the force of nature that inspired Beatrix Potter's extraordinary imagination and, in all likelihood, restored her spirits, year, after year, after year.

Roald Dahl at Gipsy House

'And above all, watch with glittering eyes the whole world around you because the greatest secrets are always hidden in the most unlikely places. Those who don't believe in magic will never find it.'

THE MINPINS

Just after the Second World War, Great Missenden, in the Chilterns, was typical of many villages in England's Home Counties. It had been largely unaffected by bombing and continued with its farming and country traditions of the previous centuries. It was a very unlikely place to attract a thirty-year-old RAF pilot whose life had encompassed ex-patriot life in Africa, a serious plane crash in the Libyan desert (in which he almost lost his life) and four years spent in the USA, meeting Walt Disney, Franklin D. Roosevelt and Ernest Hemingway. But Roald Dahl was no ordinary veteran of the Second World War, and his arrival in Great Missenden would mean that this village would never be 'ordinary' again.

Roald, who became one of the greatest children's authors on both sides of the Atlantic, might well have settled in New York, Hollywood or London. He knew Ian Fleming, who went on to write the James Bond books, and the intelligence circles he had been moving in might well have led him to a different life. He was more than 1.75m/6ft tall, dashing and handsome, and could have held his own in London's literary world, but after years of moving in political and show-business circles he was hankering for a simpler life. By the late 1940s he was already a successful author. His book *Gremlins* (an adult story

RIGHT Gipsy House in Buckinghamshire was the home of writer Roald Dahl for more than thirty years.
OPPOSITE *Allium hollandicum* 'Purple Sensation' thrives in front of the Lime Avenue, which leads to Roald's writing hut.

about the sprites that RAF pilots blamed for any mechanical failure in their planes) had almost been made into a Hollywood film, and his short stories were widely read in the USA. But the signs were already there that Roald – who had grown up on a Welsh farm with his Norwegian mother and sisters – would choose a different path. His elder sister had died at the age of seven, and his father shortly afterwards, quite possibly of a broken heart.

From the beginning, Roald felt that he needed to care for his sisters and mother – and, still unmarried, he decided to come

home. 'Home', at first, was his mother's sixteenth-century, thatched cottage in Ludgershall. Roald identified with Matthew Arnold's poem 'The Scholar-Gypsy', and the idea of being in touch with the earth was one that attracted him deeply. His interest in gardening was developing; he grew vegetables to eke out his small RAF invalid pension, bred greyhounds and set himself up as a full-time writer. Yet he was often restless and, after a trip to the States, he arrived back in the spring of 1954 newly married to actress Patricia Neal.

The newly-weds bought a small cottage called Little Whitefield on the edge of Great Missenden and moved in on 27 July 1954. They were entranced – Roald would live there for the rest of his life. In

BELOW The gardens at Gipsy House are at their peak in late spring.

THE WRITER'S GARDEN

A Writer at Work

Roald had his brick hut built in the garden of Gipsy House as a quiet place in which to work, away from his children and animal-filled household. It was lined with polystyrene for insulation and was split into two 'rooms' – an anteroom and an inner writing room, in which he sat in an old armchair with a baize-covered writing board on his knees. This was the only writing position he found comfortable, because of his long history of back problems following his plane crash in the Second World War. Roald would write in longhand, using only Dixon Ticonderoga pencils and lined, yellow legal pads, which had to be imported from the USA and the cost deducted by his American agent from his royalty statements. For his entire life, he refused to write with anything else, complaining that other pencils were too hard, too soft or did not have the right erasers on the top.

In the hut, Roald was master of his own universe. The curtains would be drawn to keep out distractions, and the room filled with objects and pictures that sparked his memory and his imagination. For thirty-six years he wrote some of the best-known children's books in publishing history there – and never wanted to write anywhere else.

The hut still stands in the garden where it has always been, but the contents have been moved, piece by piece, and its interior recreated at the Roald Dahl Museum and Story Centre in the village of Great Missenden.

ABOVE RIGHT Roald Dahl (1916–90) always worked on a baize-covered board perched on his knees.
RIGHT The writing hut was Roald's escape from busy family life at Gipsy House.

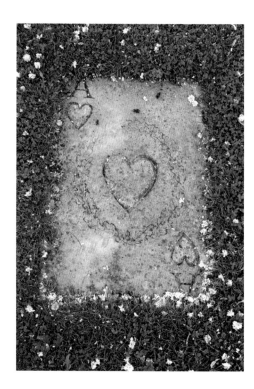

one of his 'Ideas Books' he noted how much there was to do in the garden – seeing to the roses, painting the outhouses and picking the cherries on the trees. He built himself a writing hut in the garden, where he could work uninterrupted.

Between her acting commitments, Patricia gave birth to daughters Olivia and Tessa and a son Theo, and it was here, in this Buckinghamshire family idyll, that Roald would discover his gift for storytelling to children. He knew his own children were fascinated by creatures – the Dahls kept a menagerie of rabbits, hens, dogs and tortoises – but he did not want to copy Beatrix Potter or any other writers he admired. Instead, he studied his own fruit orchard and the creatures that crawled on to the fruit and came up with the idea of making a child the same size as the worms and caterpillars – the result was *James and the Giant Peach*.

A Place for Children

The garden soon sported several features that symbolized Roald's newfound happiness. His writing hut became a sanctuary from an increasingly busy household, and he also acquired a traditional gipsy caravan from his sister. She had bought it from a gipsy who had fallen on hard times. It was a great playhouse for the children, but it was also, according to Roald's biographer Donald Sturrock, a symbol of his fascination with the freedom of the gipsy life, and the freedom to be a writer. Shortly afterwards, he renamed Little Whitefield 'Gipsy House'.

Increasingly, the garden was a setting for games with his children, inventing stories about the trees in the garden, growing vegetables and planting species roses. His eldest daughter, Olivia, learned to identify all the roses and recite their Latin names.

But the idyll was not to last. In December 1960 their son Theo was knocked out of his pram by a speeding taxi in New York and thereafter suffered years of hospitalization and surgery. Then in winter 1962 Olivia died suddenly of measles. She was aged only seven – the same age at which Roald's own sister had died.

Characteristically, it was plants and Roald's interest in plants that helped him during this time. He sought advice from alpine

ABOVE The octagonal birdhouse was once home to Roald's homing budgerigars, which were let out to fly free during the day. It is now used as a decorative glasshouse.

LEFT The Gipsy Caravan crops up in several of Roald Dahl's books, including *Danny The Champion of the World*.

OPPOSITE LEFT The gardens peaks in early summer, with a host of different poppies including *Papaver orientale* 'Patty's Plum'.

OPPOSITE CENTRE AND OPPOSITE The garden at Gipsy House has several quirky artefacts including a pair of stone American eagles outside the birdhouse (opposite centre) and a playing card that covers a utilities access point (opposite).

expert Valerie Finnis, and in the churchyard he planted a tiny rock garden with more than two hundred plants. Day after day, he would weed and tend this miniature world of rare plants next to Olivia's grave, which is inscribed: 'She stands before me as a living child' – a quotation from W.B. Yeats.

Life had to go on, and the Dahls had two more daughters, Ophelia and Lucy. Roald became fascinated with orchids and spent summer 1963 in Honolulu (where Patricia was filming with John Wayne), searching for phalaenopsis to take back to his new Orchid House – a group of plants that became a lifelong study.

He wrote frenetically – film scripts, plays, short stories and a string of successful children's books including *Charlie and the Chocolate Factory* and *Fantastic Mr Fox*. Set in the woods just beyond his house, Mr Fox battles with adversity to bring his family safely through troubled times – just as Roald was doing at Gipsy House. But by the early 1970s his marriage to Patricia was falling apart, and he had fallen in love with Felicity Crosland, who would become his wife in 1983.

Child at Heart

Through all the ups and downs, Roald never lost his inner child or his love for the garden. For his younger daughters, he invented a Big Friendly Giant who lived in the orchard, and this giant would go on to appear in *Danny The Champion of the World* (which also featured the gipsy caravan) and in his later book *The BFG*.

Whenever he was tired or disillusioned with the literary world, Roald would turn to the garden. After finishing *Danny*, he gardened non-stop for nine months. And, after receiving criticism of his work, he would just immerse himself in cultivating his orchids until he felt more like writing again.

In his later years, Roald was a creature of habit. By then, he had lived at Gipsy House for more than thirty years and he relished the routine of walking through the garden to his writing hut, tending his orchids in the greenhouse and eating good food and drinking good

ABOVE LEFT AND LEFT The path through the box Maze (above left) is paved with inscriptions taken from Roald Dahl's children's stories such as these ones (left) from an incantation in *Esio Trot*.

wine with his family. Near to the grave of his daughter Olivia, and close to his sisters and the Chiltern countryside and woods that he loved, Roald had found a kind of peace. People who knew him say he was funny, irascible and often set out to shock. The complexity of the man was something that could perhaps only be expressed through his gardening and his writing.

When Felicity came to live at Gipsy House, the greenhouse and swimming pool were replaced by a new guest annexe, and the garden was redesigned. Roald accepted that he was physically unable to work in it any more. One of his last projects was to oversee the building of a new Walled Garden, and to appoint a gardener who is still involved in the garden.

Felicity Dahl and the family continue to live in and care for Gipsy House and the garden Roald created. In the twenty-five years since Roald's death in 1990 many things have changed: the clipped box has been replaced with yew, because it is much more resilient to dog damage; hostas have been planted under the Lime Walk; and the Maze has been installed in memory of the writer and his work. But the essence of Dahl's spirit is still there, particularly the path leading under the lime trees, which he planted himself, to the old hut, where a twentieth-century genius created characters that are unlikely ever to be forgotten.

Written in Residence

GIPSY HOUSE, 1954–90 (A SELECTION)

Roald Dahl was a prolific writer best known for his children's books, which became films and stage shows.

James and the Giant Peach (1961)

Charlie and the Chocolate Factory (1964)

The Magic Finger (1966)

Fantastic Mr Fox (1970)

Danny The Champion of the World (1975)

The BFG (1982)

Matilda (1988)

The Minpins (published posthumously 1991)

Roald Dahl also wrote many short stories and the screenplays for three films: *You Only Live Twice* (1967), *Chitty Chitty Bang Bang* (1968; co-writer), and *Willy Wonka and The Chocolate Factory* (1971). His love of food is celebrated in *Memories with Food at Gipsy House* (1991), which he co-wrote with his second wife, Felicity.

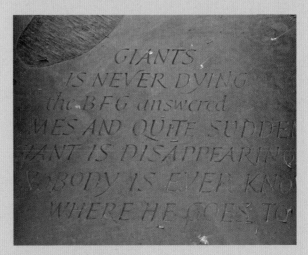

Quotation from *The BFG*

*'I have a Prospect, and
a Mulberry Tree and a
Welcome . . .'*

CHARLES DICKENS, 1858

RIGHT AND OPPOSITE When he was
a boy, Charles Dickens fell in love
with Gad's Hill Place, just outside
Rochester in Kent. As a middle-aged
man, he got the chance to buy it.

Charles Dickens at Gad's Hill Place

In *The Uncommercial Traveller*, Dickens wrote about a small boy who, passing a large, red-brick house at Gad's Hill in Kent, is told by his father that if he were to work very hard it might some day be his. The boy was Charles Dickens himself, and when his father was working at the Chatham dockyards, from 1817 to 1822, this scene might well have taken place. What we do know is that on 7 February 1855, after celebrating his forty-third birthday with friends in Gravesend, Dickens was walking back along that same road towards Rochester when he saw a 'For Sale' sign at Gad's Hill Place. He had already achieved great success with his serialized novels – *The Pickwick Papers,* his first novel, having particularly propelled him into stardom – so he had money to invest.

The family (his wife Catherine and their nine surviving children) were living in London, but Gad's Hill Place became their new summer home – and eventually Dickens's permanent residence. He paid £1,700 for the house and 4.5-hectare/11-acre grounds, plus an additional £90 to buy 0.4 hectare/1 acre of land on the south side of the road, which the family dubbed the Wilderness.

Gad's Hill Place was a fulfilment of Dickens's childhood dream, and he referred to it as his little country house, although it was clearly not some rustic cottage – and Dickens knew it. For the boy whose mother had sent him to work in a blacking factory (an experienced echoed in *David Copperfield*, but something Dickens never talked about to his friends or children), who had coped with a father frequently in debt and who had lived in some of the worst slums in London, Gad's Hill Place meant more to Dickens than a little country house.

It stands on a hill outside Rochester, although there would have been fewer trees and buildings than there are now, so Dickens would have been able to look down over the town. The road passing the house was very busy, with 60–70 coaches a day, as well as troops and naval personnel on their way to and from the garrisons and naval dockyard in Chatham.

Dickens started work on the property as soon as he had taken possession of it in 1856, enlarging the drawing room, adding extra bedrooms for the family and servants, a school room for the boys and planting lime trees along the road in front of the house, for privacy. There were great works to be done on the drains and improving the water supply by sinking a borehole and installing pumps for a well. The costs were tremendous, and Dickens, who always worried about money, decided to do public readings to help pay for the upkeep.

Dickens and his Garden

There was always something going on at Gad's Hill Place, although Dickens earmarked the room to the side of the front door as his library and eventually his quiet study. At Christmas 1864, his guests were inveigled into accompanying him down to Higham station to collect a gift from his actor friend Charles Fechter. It was a two-storey, genuine Swiss chalet – flat-packed in ninety-four pieces – and the guests helped haul it up to the house by horse and cart.

Dickens had the chalet erected at the end of a walk in the Wilderness – the plot of land across the road from the house, which, by then, plans show had become a carefully laid out Shrubbery, with straight and curving paths. To reach the Wilderness, Dickens built a tunnel under the busy Gravesend to Rochester road, to ensure private access. The tunnel still exists – although the Wilderness now has private housing and gardens built on it.

Every morning before starting work, Dickens would walk around the house and grounds carrying a hammer, nails and trowel. He was meticulous about things being tidy and well kept. Anything he could mend or put right he would; if he could not, he would make a note for the gardener, Charles Barber. Barber had come to Gad's Hill Place from Tavistock House (recommended to Dickens by his good friend Joseph Paxton) and had remained there until his retirement, when he was replaced by George Brunt. The gardener lived in the cottage in the grounds of Gad's Hill Place.

Although the gardens have undergone much upheaval since Dickens lived there, the basic layout is still discernible. In the front drive, there was a lawn and a central bed of laurels flanked by two beds for summer bedding. To one side of the house there was an Orchard and Vegetable Garden, supplying the family with produce, with an old mulberry tree at its heart. At the back, there was a raised formal terrace of lawn and borders looking over a hayfield, which provided two crops a year for his horses. Dickens soon hankered after more land, and in 1868 acquired 5.5 hectares/14 acres of meadow, at the back of the house.

Plenty of evidence indicates that Dickens loved his garden, and strove to improve it. There was a vinery, which he heated for his tender plants, and a croquet lawn. Most important to Dickens, however, was the use of colour in the planting schemes. Beneath both ground-floor bay windows he put up staging for a 'Geranium Theatre' in which he grew ranks of bright red *Pelargonium* 'Mrs Pollock'. He always wore one in his buttonhole, and buttonholes were made up for dinner guests. Dickens's daughter Katey is said to have believed that when her father became an angel he would wear

ABOVE RIGHT Dickens built a tunnel to access his writing chalet on the other side of the Gravesend to Rochester road.
RIGHT The Swiss chalet at Gad's Hill Place has been moved to Eastgate House in Rochester.

a wreath of geraniums (*Pelargonium*) and wings made from mirror glass – a reference to the fact that he installed numerous mirrors to bring light into the house.

Since his early days at Gad's Hill Place, Dickens had wanted to add a conservatory, but it was only the influx of funds from his last reading tour of America, in 1867–8, that enabled him eventually to build it. The Victorian craze for ferns and tender plants was at its height, and his fascination with them was shared by his eldest daughter Mamie. Ferns – including two very expensive tree ferns (*Dicksonia antarctica* and *Cyathea dealbata*) – were bought locally, from Mr Illman's nursery in Strood. Dickens constantly fretted about costs and warned George Brunt, soon after his arrival at Gad's Hill Place, not to order more plants than absolutely necessary. He did, however, permit him to buy eighteen more *Pelargonium* 'Mrs Pollock' and twelve lavender plants.

A Different Life

Gad's Hill Place became Dickens's home in a way no other house had done. He enjoyed playing the country squire: there were croquet and cricket matches in summer; and 'Dickensian' parties with food, drink, piano-playing by his daughter Mamie and lots of parlour games in winter. Dickens would guide visitors around Rochester cathedral or take them on tours around the Kent countryside, to see the hop fields.

But buying Gad's Hill Place also marked a major crossroads in Dickens's public and private life. He had fallen out of love with London, and two years after buying the house he separated from his wife Catherine. He had begun a relationship with Ellen Ternan, which he was forced to keep hidden from his public, and he was working harder and harder, undertaking gruelling speaking tours around Britain and in America. He was increasingly financially responsible for members of his family and worried constantly that he had not enough income – Mr Micawber's famous words about income and expenditure were an echo of his own obsession with paying his way. Many of the books he worked on at Gad's Hill Place – *A Tale of Two Cities*, *Great Expectations* and *Our Mutual Friend*, along with his unfinished last work *The Mystery of Edwin Drood* – are noticeably darker than some of his earlier works.

Literary Connections

Charles Dickens was said to be able to quote all Shakespeare's plays by heart and always carried a pocket book of the playwright's verse. The inn opposite Dickens's house is called the Sir John Falstaff (after the story in Shakespeare's *Henry IV Part I*, in which Gad's Hill was the site where Falstaff plotted with his friends to rob rich pilgrims on their way to Canterbury). It may have been one of the reasons Dickens bought the house. He later acquired some wooden furniture from a sale at Shakespeare's Stratford house and had it made into benches and a post box for the front porch of Gad's Hill Place.

The post box and bench in the front porch

Written in Residence

Charles Dickens's prolific output – producing his books in monthly instalments of anything between 7,000 and 20,000 words – stretched across his entire adult life. He wrote with a quill pen (favouring bright blue ink) on rough sheets of paper, which he folded and tore in half before starting to write on each 'slip', as he called them.

A Tale of Two Cities (1859)

Great Expectations (1860–61)

The Uncommercial Traveller (1860–70;

thirty-seven short 'papers')

Our Mutual Friend (1864–5)

The Mystery of Edwin Drood (1870)

Charles Dickens (1812–70) at work

When Dickens wanted calm and seclusion to write, he retreated to the Swiss chalet in the Wilderness. He told his friend Charles Fechter that he had never worked anywhere better, and on 25 May 1868, in a letter to his friend Mrs Annie Fields in America, he described how the chalet gave him a feeling of lightness: 'My room is up among the branches of the trees; and the birds and the butterflies fly in and out and the green branches shoot in at the open windows, and the lights and shadows of the clouds come and go with the rest of the company.'

The conservatory at Gad's Hill Place was finished just two days before Dickens died. On the evening of 7 June 1870 he was determined to hang up the Chinese lanterns that had just been sent down from London. He collapsed from a stroke the next day and died on 9 June.

Katey subsequently recalled an evening during those last few precious days at Gad's Hill Place, when they sat in the conservatory with the lamps turned down low, and the perfume of the flowers in the garden coming in through the open windows. A 'light' was about to go out, not only for her but also for thousands, even millions, of Dickens's followers.

Gad's Hill Place after Dickens

Dickens's will decreed that Gad's Hill Place be sold. It was bought by his eldest son, Charley, who lived there with his wife Bessie.

They welcomed back Dickens's wife, Catherine, after the long estrangement. In time, the property went out of the family, the Swiss chalet was moved to Cobham Hall and eventually found a permanent home in Rochester in the grounds of Eastgate House, which appeared in *The Mystery of Edwin Drood* as The Nun's House.

Gad's Hill Place then had several owners until, in 1923, it was acquired by Mr Burt for his three daughters to establish a boarding school for girls. It remains a school to this day, although it is now an independent school for day pupils. The school no longer uses the house in which Dickens lived, and a trust has been formed to raise funds to turn the house into a Dickens heritage centre. However, restoration of the grounds and restocking of the furniture, which now lies in other collections, will be a big task.

OPPOSITE ABOVE Dickens's study was sketched by S.L. Fildes in 1871, a year after his death.
RIGHT TOP *Rosa banksiae* 'Lutea' grows on the back of the house.
RIGHT CENTRE The conservatory was finished only days before Dickens died.
RIGHT BOTTOM Dickens chose and hung the lamps in the conservatory himself. It was filled with tree ferns, palms, phormiums, myrtle, fuchsias, pelargoniums and a large collection of ferns.

Virginia Woolf at Monk's House

'It's an unpretending house, long and low, a house of many doors,
on one side fronting the street of Rodmell, and wood-boarded on that side.'

VIRGINIA WOOLF, 1919

Those who make the pilgrimage through the tiny lanes of Rodmell, near Lewes, on the south coast of England, in search of Virginia Woolf find themselves outside a simple, weatherboarded cottage with roses clambering over the facade. It is warm and welcoming, and seems somehow too cosy to be the home of the brilliant, but troubled, writer who took her own life at the age of fifty-nine.

Virginia and Leonard Woolf bought Monk's House in 1919. They had been living nearby, at Asheham House, which Virginia had rented (and loved) as a weekend escape from town. They went to auction and bid £700 for the house and garden, which stand next to the village church. At first, Virginia was not impressed by the house, but all her objections 'were forced to yield place to a profound pleasure at the size and shape and fertility and wildness of the garden'.

When Virginia and Leonard arrived, the garden was 0.3 hectare / ¾ acre, to the back and side of the house, with fruit trees and a vegetable patch. They were always meticulous about recording who paid for what, and, because Virginia had just published her novel *The Voyage Out*, she paid for one of the first areas to be built at Monk's House – the Italian Garden.

At first, Virginia worked in an outbuilding above the laundry, but by 1921 she was telling her sister, Vanessa Bell, who lived at nearby Charleston, about the new garden room that was being made out of

RIGHT *Rosa* 'Félicité Perpétue' spills over the wall at the front of Monk's House in Sussex.
OPPOSITE From her writing hut in the garden, Virginia Woolf could look out across the bowling lawn to the South Downs.

THE WRITER'S GARDEN

THE WRITER'S GARDEN

an old tool house. This became known as The Lodge. Some years later, when Virginia and Leonard acquired another stretch of land looking over to Caburn Hill and the South Downs, The Lodge was moved up to the Orchard, to make the best of the view. The cost of building the hut, with its wooden-clad sides and shingle roof, was £157, which Virginia thought was well worth it. She often slept there on warm summer nights.

On the new land, too, a level bowling green was made, where weekend visitors would play bowls and croquet. Below, they put in an elliptical pond, built of concrete, to fit in with the dew ponds found all across the Downs. The Woolfs also named two elm trees on the boundary – one 'Virginia' and the other 'Leonard' – and asked for their ashes to be sprinkled under them when they died.

A Gardener's Garden

Both Virginia and Leonard loved the garden. Although her diaries record helping with the weeding and seed sowing, it was progressively Leonard who did most of the planning, pruning, planting and building of terraces and ponds. In 1926 he took on a full-time gardener, Percy Bartholomew, who would stay with Leonard until 1945.

Percy had to tend a large vegetable garden, which grew produce for the house, and the surplus was given away to villagers or sold at Lewes market. There were five hives for honey, an extensive collection of soft fruit – strawberries, raspberries and currants – and an orchard of apples, pears, quince and medlars. Percy's daughter Marie remembers Leonard helping her father to prune the fruit trees and to collect the honey. In autumn, Leonard would collect the windfall apples from their orchard and take a basket to the village school just over the wall.

ABOVE LEFT Wherever you walk in the garden, the village church spire in Rodmell is always visible.
BELOW FAR LEFT, BELOW CENTRE LEFT, BELOW LEFT Aged terracotta urns, bird tables and stone pots are set among the plants in the cottage garden at Monk's House.
RIGHT TOP, RIGHT CENTRE AND RIGHT BOTTOM Virginia's writing hut, known as The Lodge (right top and right centre), is away from the main house and offered her a measure of peace. In front, the flat lawn was used to play bowls and croquet, and had a lovely view across the South Downs (right bottom).

The place that Virginia loved perhaps best of all was the orchard. Her short story 'The Orchard' is about a girl who wakes to find herself in an apple orchard very much like the one at Monk's House. The girl hears the sound of children playing, which you can still do today.

Leonard liked the garden to be wild, with everything fighting for space, but his taste was for bold colours – kniphofias and dahlias – rather than pastel pinks. He became a plantsman through interest and study, and planted a large *Trachycarpus fortunei* near the house, and interesting shrubs including laburnum, magnolia, campsis, chimonanthus and three *Ginkgo biloba* (though only two remain). Virginia disapproved of Leonard spending large sums of money on the garden – and dismissed his three greenhouses as 'Leonard's Crystal Palaces'. Leonard was a passionate collector of cacti and tropical plants, and the boilers for the greenhouses had to be continually stoked by the gardener when the Woolfs were away.

A Writer's Garden

After their London flat was bombed, the Woolfs moved all their possessions to Monk's House in 1940, and Sussex became their permanent home. While Leonard threw himself into the practical running of the garden, for Virginia it was a backdrop, a landscape, for her thoughts and her writing. She loved to walk through the flower gardens and pick flowers for the house, but mostly she wandered or sat and read in this peaceful place. She wrote in her diary: 'Never has the garden been so lovely – all ablaze even now; dazzling one's eyes with reds & pinks & purples & mauves; the carnations in great bunches, the roses lit like lamps.'

On a quiet day, Virginia would write and correct proofs in The Lodge if it was warm enough. Then, in the afternoon, she would walk out on to the Downs and back in time for tea at four, followed by letter writing and her diary, which she did rigorously – as did Leonard. The ritual of walking across the garden to reach her writing hut kept her in close contact with the garden.

Very often, the house was full of witty and interesting people, and Virginia generally delighted in it. Their visitors were mainly members of the Bloomsbury Circle – her sister Vanessa, Vanessa's husband Clive Bell and the children Julian, Quentin and Angelica, the painter Duncan Grant, John Maynard Keynes and Lytton Strachey

THE WRITER'S GARDEN

– along with favoured friends such as T.S. Elliot, E.M. Forster and Vita Sackville-West.

A Moment in Time

After Virginia's death, Leonard continued to live at Monk's House, adding on the conservatory at the back of the house in the 1950s, when he allowed his greenhouses be taken down. His companion in later years was the American painter Trekkie Ritchie Parsons, and he built on an extension to The Lodge as a studio for her.

When Leonard died, Trekkie became the custodian of Monk's House, and in 1980 it was taken on by The National Trust. The house no longer has live-in tenants, and the house and gardens are

ABOVE *Rosa* 'Belvedere' cascades outside Virginia's bedroom window at Monk's House.

OPPOSITE ABOVE The shape of the concrete pool was meant to echo the circular dew ponds found in this part of Sussex.

OPPOSITE BELOW The Italian Garden, with its urns and statues, was Virginia's contribution to the garden.

RIGHT The Orchard was Virginia Woolf's favourite part of the garden.

BELOW LEFT A life-size, terracotta cast of Diana stands outside the Painting Studio , built on to The Lodge for the American painter Trekkie Parsons.

BELOW CENTRE Leonard Woolf kept bees and collected honey from the hives in the Orchard.

BELOW RIGHT Monk's House Kitchen Garden is shared with local allotment holders.

THE WRITER'S GARDEN

now open fully to visitors. Some of the original trees are still there, but many others have been added over the years. The elms are sadly no longer there – the one known as 'Virginia' blew down in a gale in 1943, and 'Leonard' succumbed to Dutch elm disease in 1985.

In the Orchard, the long grass beneath the trees with paths mown through is not quite how Leonard kept it. He had it mowed to exactly 7cm/3in high, with the edges and paths mowed lower for walking – known as 'step mowing'. This, along with the beehives, is something that the National Trust may reintroduce over the coming years.

Mainly, though, the garden is as Leonard and Virginia intended it – in Virginia's twenty-two years there and Leonard's fifty. On a summer's day, the paths are overhung with plants in that semi-wild state that Virginia loved. The Italian Garden is a cool, green space out of the heat, and the bowling lawn still welcomes those who want to play games, against the backdrop of the South Downs. The Vegetable Garden is cultivated, and part of its land is given to local people for use as allotments.

A house – or a garden – holds the life stories of all the people who inhabit it. But when Virginia Woolf chose this sleepy corner of Sussex, her story is surely the one that will be retold again, and again.

Written in Residence

MONK'S HOUSE, 1919–41

After Virginia Woolf died, in 1941, Leonard lived on at Monk's House until 1969.

Mrs Dalloway (1925)
To the Lighthouse (1927)
Orlando: A Biography (1929
A Room of One's Own (1929)
The Waves (1931)
The Years (1937)

Bust of Virginia Woolf (1882–1941) by Stephen Tomlin (1931)

Winston Churchill at Chartwell

Writer, historian, artist and statesman Sir Winston Spencer Churchill was probably never happier than when working outdoors, making water gardens, repairing buildings or putting up walls. It was a side of Britain's most famous prime minister that not many people saw . . . and it began at Chartwell, the Kent house and garden that became his home.

In 1921, the Churchills' youngest daughter Marigold had died at the age of two. Churchill was now seeking a home that would be not only a refuge but also a challenge, and for the next forty years Chartwell would be both.

Churchill first saw Chartwell in autumn 1922, just after his daughter Mary was born. He loved it unconditionally, right from the start, but his wife Clementine, known as Clemmie, had serious reservations about the house – which needed total renovation – as well as the costs of running a 32-hectare/80-acre estate. This was a time when the Churchills were not financially secure. Churchill, who had been a Liberal MP, failed to get re-elected to Parliament at the 1923 general election, and at the age of forty-seven he was facing an uncertain future.

For Churchill, the gloomy, dilapidated state of the old manor house paled into insignificance besides its glorious setting. Sheltered by beech woods and with far-reaching views over the Weald of Kent, it captivated him. However, he was even more excited by the possibilities offered by the natural watercourses: the springs of the Chart well rise at the top of the garden and feed the lakes. Churchill, who had grown up looking out on the 'Capability' Brown lakes of Blenheim Palace, saw an opportunity to make water features that might rival those of his childhood home. It was this landscape that really fed his imagination and meant that, whether or not it was sensible, he was determined to buy it.

'The days have slipped away very quickly here. I have passed them almost entirely in the open air, making a dam . . .'

WINSTON CHURCHILL, 1925

RIGHT A sculpture of Winston and Clementine Churchill by Oscar Nemon stands by the Lower Lake.
OPPOSITE Chartwell in Kent was Churchill's home for more than forty years.

Now that he was on the sidelines of political life, Churchill decided to provide for his family – and keep Chartwell going – by his writing. For the next seventeen years, until the outbreak of the Second World War, in 1939, he wrote a stream of speeches, newspaper articles and books on biography and history, most notably about his famous ancestor John Churchill, 1st Duke of Marlborough and the hero of Blenheim – the battle that gave its name to Churchill's childhood home, Blenheim Palace. He also began writing the epic *History of the English-Speaking Peoples*, although it would not be finished and published until after the Second World War.

Building the Dream

Churchill appointed the architect Philip Tilden to redesign the interior of the house and the grounds. Tilden set about removing the ivy from the walls and a bank of rhododendrons that were encroaching and making the house dark and damp. He added a new wing, to create more rooms overlooking the garden, and built the summer house on the terrace (later to become the Marlborough Pavilion). In 1928 Tilden designed a play-cottage for Churchill's six-year-old daughter, Mary, within the Kitchen Garden; it became known as the Marycot.

But when it came to the rest of the grounds, Churchill was determined to take it into his own hands. He first tackled the lake at the bottom of the valley, expanding it – perhaps to echo the stretches of water at Blenheim. In 1925 he told Stanley Baldwin that he had been working on the dam, 'which extends my lake and finally, I hope, removes it from the category of ponds'.

His work at Chartwell was temporarily interrupted when he was appointed Chancellor of the Exchequer in the Conservative government (he held the position from 1925 to 1929). But Churchill's brand of Edwardian oratory was out of fashion, and the Wall Street Crash of November 1929 did not help his reputation. At fifty-five, his career seemed to be over, and he began what would become known as 'the Wilderness years'.

It was a time when Chartwell and its grounds became particularly important to Churchill. He suffered from depression and would lose himself in outdoor projects – particularly the rebuilding of the walls in the Kitchen Garden. As a card-carrying member of the Amalgamated Union of Building Trade Workers, he was apparently very good at bricklaying and could lay up to ninety bricks an hour. He planted an orchard of plums, quinces, apples and pears (all acquired from George Bunyard's nursery in Maidstone), and built a tree house for the older children.

Although the Churchills welcomed a stream of visitors, there was more time for Winston to spend in the garden and to paint. He was an accomplished amateur artist and added a Studio in the 1930s to a range of cottages just above the lakes. He painted out of doors too, particularly the lakes and his Australian black swans, which were given to him by the Australian government. The Studio was well away from the main house and allowed him to paint uninterruptedly.

Chartwell's Gardens

The source of the Chart (the Chart well) is somewhere on the property but has not been definitely located. The water collects in two reservoirs behind the house and flows down into the Golden Orfe Pond – an ancient pond that Churchill rebuilt, stocked with fish and surrounded with *Gunnera manicata* and Japanese maples. The golden orfe were ordered from Harrods – another of Churchill's excesses, which Clementine probably disapproved of.

From here, the water flows through sandpits and reed beds, down a small waterfall into the swimming pool built by Tilden in the early 1930s. (It was heated by two boilers to a constant 24°C/75°F.) From the swimming pool, the water flows into the upper and lower lakes, which Churchill constantly tweaked to make look more substantial. When Clementine was away in 1935, Churchill hired an excavator and

OPPOSITE Churchill built himself a Painting Studio adjoining the cottages behind the Orchard.

RIGHT TOP AND RIGHT CENTRE A special seat and box of food were placed beside the pond so that Churchill could sit and feed his golden orfe every morning.

RIGHT BOTTOM The heated swimming pool at Chartwell was built by architect Philip Tilden. It was fed by naturally filtered spring water.

THE WRITER'S GARDEN

set about making an island – writing delightedly to his wife about how the digger sank in the mud and what a mess it all was.

With the addition of the Rose Garden in 1924, Clementine began to have a bigger say in the garden. She wanted a 'proper' flower garden. Therefore, following advice from her cousin Venetia Montagu, she had the space close to the house divided into quarters with a cross-shaped path, and each corner planted with a standard wisteria. She liked pastel colours and scent, and this is something the gardening team adhere to today in what is known as Lady Churchill's Rose Garden.

The Pavilion in the corner of the Marlborough terrace was originally a simple summer house, which again had been Clementine's idea. Churchill had a low opinion of garden houses, which he thought were overrun with spiders and woodlice. In 1927 Tilden designed an open, elegant summer house with a view down over the lower lawns and lakes, across the beech woods towards the Weald of Kent. Some two decades later, in 1949, Churchill's nephew, the artist John Spencer Churchill, painted scenes of the Battle of Blenheim on the interior walls of the building, and it was renamed the Marlborough Pavilion.

Churchill hoped that Chartwell, where he was always beset with financial difficulties, could be self-sufficient. He wrote to Clementine in 1923: 'I beg you do not worry about money . . . Chartwell is to be our home. We must make it in every way charming and as far as possible economically self-contained.' Before and during the Second World War, the Kitchen Garden was therefore an important source of produce for the household. After a long fallow period from the 1960s, when it was laid to grass, it is in full production again, supplying cut flowers, fruit and vegetables.

In 1958, on Winston and Clementine's Golden Wedding, their children installed a Golden Rose Avenue down the centre of the Walled Garden. Backed by beech hedges and with an old sundial in the centre,

ABOVE FAR LEFT *Rosa* 'Albertine' entwines the pergola in front of the house.
ABOVE LEFT *Rosa* 'Pink Parfait' flourishes in Lady Churchill's Rose Garden.
BELOW LEFT Lady Churchill's Rose Garden is where Clementine indulged her taste for pastel colours and scented roses.
ABOVE RIGHT The interior of the Marlborough Pavilion has scenes painted by Churchill's nephew, the artist John Spencer Churchill.
RIGHT *Rosa* 'Meg' climbs up the walls of the Marlborough Pavilion.

THE WRITER'S GARDEN

the parallel borders were planted with 146 standard and bush roses of twenty-eight different golden varieties – including *Rosa* 'Golden Dawn', *R.* 'Sutter's Gold' and *R.* 'Honeyglow'. Artists such as Augustus John, Vanessa Bell and John Nash were commissioned to paint each variety, and their paintings were presented to the Churchills bound in a book that can still be seen at Chartwell.

A New Chapter

When war was declared in 1939, life at Chartwell changed. The house was shut up, although Churchill would occasionally go there in times of stress, but stay in one of the cottages. When, having led Britain to victory, he was then defeated in the election of May 1945, he returned to Chartwell to wander through the overgrown grounds and consider his future. The cost of the upkeep was vast, and Churchill had no option but to put the house and estate up for sale. A group of his friends stepped in, anonymously buying the house in 1947 with the proviso that Winston and Clementine could stay in their home for the rest of their lives. It would then pass to the National Trust as a permanent memorial to the great man.

Some houses and gardens lose the spirit of their owners over time. Chartwell existed before Churchill, but the garden he created is so powerfully his own vision that it is hard to envisage it ever belonging to anyone else.

FAR LEFT TOP, FAR LEFT CENTRE AND FAR LEFT BOTTOM Among the roses in the Golden Rose Avenue are *Rosa* 'Sutter's Gold' (far left top), *R.* 'Amber Queen' (far left centre) and *R.* 'Korresia' (far left bottom).
LEFT The Golden Rose Avenue was planted for Winston and Clementine Churchills' fiftieth wedding anniversary.

Written in Residence

CHARTWELL, 1922–65
Winston Churchill was the only serving prime minister to receive the Nobel Prize for Literature, in 1953, 'for his mastery of historical and biographical description as well as for brilliant oratory in defending exalted human values'.

My Early Life (1930)
Marlborough: His Life and Times (four volumes, 1933–8)
The World Crisis (six volumes, 1923–31)
Great Contemporaries (1937)
The Second World War (six volumes, 1948–54)
A History of the English-Speaking Peoples (four volumes, from Roman Britain to 1914, 1956–8)

Winston Churchill (1874–1965) in the study at Chartwell (1953)

Laurence Sterne at Shandy Hall

'. . . everytime a man smiles – but much more so when he laughs, it adds something to this Fragment of Life.'

LAURENCE STERNE, 1760

On the road to Thirsk in North Yorkshire, if you do not drive too fast through the village of Coxwold, you might spot an ancient, crooked house with a hanging sign announcing Shandy Hall. Pull over and you might also see a plaque, just above the front door, stating that in this house the writer Laurence Sterne penned the eighteenth-century bestseller, *The Life and Opinions of Tristram Shandy, Gentleman*. Go inside the house, and you will discover the story of the man, which is every bit as intriguing as the book for which he became famous.

OPPOSITE The Barn Garden at Shandy Hall in North Yorkshire looks out towards Byland Abbey and the Hambleton Hills.

BELOW LEFT The front facade has retained the layout seen in nineteenth-century photographs, with two variegated hollies and a small box Parterre.

BELOW CENTRE The medieval 'hall' was named after Laurence Sterne's most famous creation – Tristram Shandy.

BELOW RIGHT Laurence Sterne (1713–68) was an eighteenth-century clergyman who became a bestselling comic author.

Sterne did not have the best start in life. Although his great-grandfather was Archbishop of York, his father was a poor soldier, and Laurence was born in barracks in Co. Tipperary, Ireland. Young Laurence was saved from obscurity by his wealthier Yorkshire relatives, who funded his studies at Jesus College, Cambridge and set him on the path to becoming a man of the church. He was given the living of two Yorkshire parishes (Sutton-on-the-Forest and Stillington), married a vicar's daughter (Elizabeth Lumley) and settled down to an ecclesiastical life.

He was, by all accounts, a brilliant, but very serious preacher. Yet something was niggling away at the back of his mind – a different view of life than the one everyone expected him to have. In his mid-forties, Sterne sat down and wrote the first two volumes of *Tristram Shandy* and had them self-published, anonymously, by a printer in York in 1759. This novel is a funny, irreverent tale that broke the mould of serious, worthy and often pompous writing of the mid-eighteenth century. It caused equal delight and shock, especially when the public discovered that it was written by a vicar in Yorkshire.

Sterne was a genuine overnight sensation. By the following year he was travelling to London, having his portrait painted by Joshua Reynolds, and the great William Hogarth had been commissioned to do an illustration for the second edition of *Tristram Shandy*. This was to be the very first illustration of a scene from a story in a printed book; until then, the only illustrations in novels had been portraits of the author.

Although Sterne was an obscure curate no longer, he was still a curate. In 1760 he was given the living of Coxwold and moved into the parsonage, which fronted the road to Thirsk, close to his church. It was not long before the locals were calling the house 'Shandy Hall' – 'Shandy', in the North Yorkshire dialect, meaning 'odd', something a bit off-kilter, something not-quite-right.

Shandy Hall and its Garden

Sterne was forty-six years old when he moved into Shandy Hall. He was a tall man who had suffered from tuberculosis since childhood, and was not particularly strong, but he did love to take long walks, ride and work in his garden. His wife Elizabeth had possibly suffered a nervous breakdown, and she and their daughter were spending much of their time in York. Sterne therefore, to all intents and purposes, lived alone, and the garden, his parish duties and his writing were his major occupations.

The house itself is a medieval 'hall' house, with later additions, rather than the grand manor house suggested by its name. The garden was surrounded by a stone wall, enclosing a yard, where ducks, chickens and geese ran free, and included a productive vegetable and flower garden. The whole plot was around 0.4 hectare/1 acre.

THE WRITER'S GARDEN

Its footprint has changed little in 250 years, although an additional 0.4 hectare/1 acre of woodland was added later, making the 0.8 hectare/2 acres that exist today.

With his new-found wealth, Sterne added a red-brick 'garden front' to the west of Shandy Hall. Visitors could then appreciate this slightly more genteel aspect as they approached the house, rather than enter through the yard on the other side. They would perhaps have walked under a sweet chestnut tree on the roadside

OPPOSITE FAR LEFT This early view of Shandy Hall was painted by James Ferguson.
OPPOSITE The plaque above the front door is slightly incorrect, as Sterne had written two volumes of *Tristram Shandy* before he arrived in Coxwold.
BELOW LEFT Sterne wrote the other seven of the nine volumes of *The Life and Opinions of Tristram Shandy, Gentleman* in his study.
BELOW RIGHT The 'garden front' extension was added to the original house by Sterne in the 1760s.

Written in Residence

SHANDY HALL, 1760–68

Laurence Sterne combined writing with preaching and caring for the parishioners of his Yorkshire parishes.
The Life and Opinions of Tristram Shandy, Gentleman
(nine volumes, 1759–67; the first two volumes were written at Sutton-on-the-Forest).
A Sentimental Journey through France and Italy
(two volumes, 1768)

WORK INSPIRED BY *TRISTRAM SHANDY*

Tristram Shandy was not only a funny novel, it is now recognized as being the first non-linear novel – a series of digressions, which would allow the reader to read the volumes or sections in any order. Artists in particular find much to be inspired by Sterne's work, and cartoonist Martin Rowson produced a graphic version of the novel (1996).

The story of Sterne and *Tristram Shandy* inspired the film starring Steve Coogan, *A Cock and Bull Story* (2006), which entwines the story of the writer, his creation, and the actor attempting to portray him.

First editions of *Tristram Shandy*

part of the garden – the old tree was struck by lightning in 1910 but still has a vivid presence today.

In the study at Shandy Hall, Sterne went on to write seven more volumes of *Tristram Shandy*, as well as a travelogue with a difference, called *A Sentimental Journey* – another ground-breaking work.

Sterne was no eighteenth-century gentleman of leisure. When he was not writing or editing sermons in his downstairs study he was out in the garden, where he was to be found digging or wheeling away rubbish. He was a prolific planter of fruit trees, and there are parish records from his former parish of Sutton-on-the-Forest, which record him planting an espalier apple hedge, nectarines, peaches, apples, pears, cherries and plum trees – all enclosed by a paling fence.

Towards the end of his life, in 1767, Sterne, now separated from his wife, fell in love with a twenty-three-year-old woman called Eliza Draper. She was married to an official of the East India Company in Bombay and was ordered by her husband to return to India. With promises of their mutual love, they parted, but continued to write to each other. Sterne returned to Shandy Hall an ill and heartbroken man and set about creating a room above his study for Eliza – should she one day return to him. He imagined her accompanying him on his regular walks across the fields to Byland Abbey, and cleared the brambles from the path in case she should join him. She never did.

Yet Shandy Hall revived his spirits, and he remained cheerful and wrote prodigiously. His philosophy was simple – that good physical health goes along with fun and laughter. He died in 1768 – never finishing *A Sentimental Journey*, but leaving, in *Tristram Shandy*, one of the quirkiest and cleverest works in the English language. It has never been out of print for 250 years.

A New Chapter

By the mid-1960s, Shandy Hall was an empty, forlorn house, its garden overgrown and the medieval structure in danger of decay. In 1967 the Laurence Sterne Trust was founded by Sterne scholar and enthusiast Kenneth Monkman in order to buy the building from Newburgh Priory, which owned it. Monkman became its live-in curator and, with his wife Julia, became the driving force behind the trust. Julia Monkman was also responsible for the present design of

ABOVE The 'garden front' extension is here framed by an old plum tree in which grows *Rosa* 'Albéric Barbier'.
LEFT To the side of the house, an arcade has been made from old outhouses.

the gardens. A public appeal to save Shandy Hall was launched – to which Henry Moore gave a sculpture to be sold and J.B. Priestley wrote a special essay to help with the appeal.

The garden at Shandy Hall today is abundant, slightly eccentric and quite wild, which echoes Sterne's Shandy-esque view of the world. The philosophy behind the planting is to make it as biodiverse as possible – many of the perennials are single species or simple cultivars that attract butterflies and bees. In the woodland section, native wild flowers and cultivated plants are allowed to battle it out – the gardener only intervening when hogweed, nettles or brambles seem to be dominating. Studies of moths in the garden

have revealed more than 300 different species, including the Smoky Wainscot and Muslin Footman – names that an eighteenth-century naturalist would have recognized.

The garden is not a recreation of how Sterne would have had it, nor is it trying to preserve a particular moment in time. Nevertheless, fans of Sterne will pick up on several visual references to his life and work. The greengage tree alludes to the fact that *Tristram Shandy* contained the first mention of the tree in English literature. A marble-leaved nasturtium at the foot of the barn wall is a nod to Sterne's marbled page in *Tristram Shandy*. The decorative iron railings represent Sterne's 'squiggles' – when he

wanted to illustrate how the plot of his book was taking a strange and interesting turn, he literally drew curly lines on the page – another first in printing and literature.

In 2002 Patrick Wildgust took over as curator. He has since built up the educational side of the trust's work while his partner, Chris Pearson, tends the gardens. In the house – built originally in 1430 – medieval wall paintings have been uncovered behind the Georgian panelling, and there is an unrivalled collection of Sterne's books, paintings, manuscripts and ephemera. New life is blowing through the old timbers, with a gallery, a programme of arts and creative workshops, and a secondhand bookshop. Although funds are still needed to ensure the future, the house and gardens are thriving, and visitors are charmed by its lived-in feel and the story of its extraordinary incumbent.

ABOVE LEFT This old sweet chestnut was hit by lightning in 1910.
ABOVE CENTRE The perennial sweet pea *Lathyrus latifolius* jostles for space with *Brachyglottis* 'Sunshine' near the west front.
ABOVE RIGHT The curled iron railings at Shandy Hall are by artist–blacksmith Chris Topp.
OPPOSITE FAR LEFT The old quarry is now a Wild Garden with stands of ash trees.
OPPOSITE Rambling roses, including *Rosa* 'Rambling Rector', are allowed to grow freely in the Wild Garden.

*'Unless you are in haste
and elsewhere bound,
You may as well come in.
I'll shew you round.'*

BERNARD SHAW'S
RHYMING PICTURE GUIDE
TO AYOT ST LAWRENCE

RIGHT Yellow achilleas and
veronicastrums flourish in the
perennial summer borders
at George Bernard Shaw's
Hertfordshire garden.
OPPOSITE ABOVE The locals in Ayot
St Lawrence renamed the house
'Shaw's Corner', and it has been
know by this name ever since.
OPPOSITE The red-brick house was
built in 1902, and the Shaws bought
it in 1906.

George Bernard Shaw at Shaw's Corner

The Shaws – George Bernard and his wife Charlotte – moved into their red-brick home in Ayot St Lawrence in 1906. They had been house-hunting for some time, as they wanted a retreat away from (but not too far from) London's theatreland. The story goes that in the Ayot St Lawrence churchyard Shaw discovered the tombstone of a seventy-year-old woman with the inscription 'Her time was short,' and he reckoned that, if seventy years was considered short in this part of the world, this would be just the place for him to settle.

The locals in this tiny village were suspicious. Shaw was already a celebrated playwright, drama and critic; he was also a socialist and was Irish. But he became an accepted member of the community soon after the area suffered its worst blizzard in history, in 1915, and Shaw went out and helped the local men to saw up trees and clear the roads. From then on, the locals insisted on calling his house Shaw's Corner, by which name it has been known since.

From Shaw's Corner, Shaw would continue his amazing literary output of plays, political pamphlets and prose. He had a study in the main house, where he answered correspondence with his secretary, but every day he would walk down to the bottom of the garden to his revolving writing shed. Here he worked for the next forty-four years on some of the great plays of the twentieth century – including *Pygmalion* and *Saint Joan*.

The Shaws used the house as a country retreat, spending weekends up in London attending performances and working on plays, and coming down to Ayot St Lawrence in the middle of the week. Gradually, they spent more time here and, in later life, Shaw rarely left. The gardens and grounds were their sanctuary – a place for relaxation and exercise. Charlotte and George Bernard would walk a certain route around the garden every day, piling up stones in a heap to mark each kilometre they had walked – putting one stone on the pile every time they passed it.

All the evidence confirms that the Shaws were very proud of their garden. Charlotte was the housekeeper – the one who ordered and paid the bills – and she spent substantial sums of money on delphinium seeds from Suttons and sacks of tulip bulbs and irises, which arrived by train at Wheathampstead station. She wrote letters to nurseries and sent samples of plants to be identified.

The Shaws were new gardeners, but very keen ones and relied on the help of their head gardener, Henry Higgs, who stayed with them until 1943, when he was replaced by Fred Drury, the under-gardener. On the bookshelf in the study was a copy of Gertrude Jekyll's *Gardens*

for Small Country Houses, and they began to get ideas for making a garden in this virtually empty plot. Yews were planted in the drive, along with cedars and beech in the grounds and a *Magnolia grandiflora* on the south side of the house. They put in new herbaceous borders in the 'country-house' style with lilies, delphiniums and poppies, made a Rose Dell and dug a huge vegetable plot (Shaw was a well-known vegetarian) to provide for their needs – although the produce they grew was often given away in the village. They kept bees and planted an orchard.

To reflect the success of his play about Joan of Arc, Shaw put up a statue of St Joan above the Rose Dell. He called her the Maid of Orleans and said that she was deliberately sculpted without banner, sword or armour. He preferred to see her as the daughter of a farmer, rather than as a warrior figure.

In 1920 the Shaws bought extra land from their friend Apsley Cherry-Garrard, who had inherited the neighbouring estate of Lamer Park. This additional land made the Shaws' garden up to 1.4 hectares / 3½ acres, and it now included glorious views over the surrounding Hertfordshire countryside.

A Sociable Place

Shaw's Corner reflects the struggle between the public personality and the reclusive writer. Shaw loved nothing more than hiding away in his hut or sawing logs for the fire, yet made time for his visitors. They included the writer and traveller T.E. Lawrence ('Lawrence of Arabia'), who would arrive on one of his Brough Superior motorcycles, H.G. Wells and Vivien Leigh, who came to rehearse on the lawn for the 1945 film version of *Caesar and Cleopatra*. Most Sundays, the Shaws would walk over the fields and along the Lime

LEFT George Bernard Shaw (1856–1950) talking to his neighbour, the artist Stephen Winsten. Stephen's wife Clare was the sculptor of the statue of St Joan.
RIGHT ABOVE The Shaws were aiming for a country-house garden, which featured lilies, stachys and roses.
FAR RIGHT ABOVE The statue of St Joan by Clare Winsten stands above the Rose Dell.
RIGHT *Rosa* Gertrude Jekyll perfectly suits the early twentieth-century style of the garden.
FAR RIGHT Every day, Shaw and his wife Charlotte walked through the garden, passing the rose beds.

Avenue at Lamer Park to have lunch with Cherry-Garrard and his wife. Cherry-Garrard was suffering from his experiences as part of Scott's expedition to the Antarctic, and Shaw helped him with his writing of *The Worst Journey in the World*.

There were also social and political gatherings at Shaw's Corner. While sitting out on the south-facing terrace – nicknamed 'the Riviera' – in their deckchairs, they would discuss literature, art and socialism. In 1926 Shaw famously refused to take the money for his Nobel Prize for Literature, giving it instead to the newly created Anglo-Swedish Literary Foundation.

A Living Showplace

Shaw planned what would happen to the house after his death. As he had no children, he arranged for the National Trust to take over Shaw's Corner in its entirety, ensuring that his unique collection of ephemera – from his Oscar statuette to his collection of tools – should be preserved for the future. Shaw wanted the house to be a living showplace of his life's work, not a 'dead museum'.

In true Shavian fashion, Shaw died after a fall in the garden – he was pruning a greengage tree at the age of ninety-four. His hope, that he would live a long time in this part of rural England, had been fulfilled. His ashes were – as he wished – mixed with Charlotte's and scattered along the footpaths of the garden they had walked together.

After his death, the garden was mainly turfed over for ease of maintenance, but it has since been restored, recreating the historical layout of the beds shown on early twentieth-century photographs. In the Orchard, some of the old trees survive, but new plums, pears, quince, apples and damsons have been added, and it is thriving again. The vegetable area is necessarily much smaller than it was in its heyday, but is still a garden that the Shaws might well have recognized as theirs. And Shaw would probably be pleased to know that Shaw's Corner is still alive with people. Each year, around the time of his birthday in July, performances of his plays are put on in the garden.

RIGHT ABOVE Shaw's writing hut originally came from a tuberculosis sanitorium. It revolves, to make the best of the natural light.
RIGHT Shaw dealt with his correspondence in the house, but always wrote his plays in the hut.
BELOW LEFT Shaw was a noted vegetarian, and the Vegetable Garden was much larger in his day.
BELOW The Orchard at Shaw's Corner has been replanted with plum, quince, apple and damson trees.

Written in Residence

SHAW'S CORNER, 1906–50

George Bernard Shaw was born in Dublin and moved to London at the age of twenty and had written many successful plays before he came to Shaw's Corner. He had impressed royalty: King Edward VII reputedly fell off his chair laughing at a production of *John Bull's Other Island*; and the prime minister had attended the first night of *Major Barbara* in 1905. But Shaw's 'country' phase would be equally, if not more productive: thirty-eight out of his total output of fifty-two plays were written at Shaw's Corner including:

Androcles and the Lion (1912)

Pygmalion (1912; made into a film 1938; later became the musical *My Fair Lady*)

Heartbreak House (1919)

Back to Methuselah (1921)

Saint Joan (1923; for which Shaw won the Nobel Prize for Literature)

The Millionairess (1936)

He also wrote on political theory, including *The Intelligent Woman's Guide to Socialism and Capitalism* (1928).

Shaw was a prolific photographer and used his photos to compile *Bernard Shaw's Rhyming Picture Guide to Ayot St Lawrence* – the village that had become his home. In it were black and white images showing the young orchard and the house clad with creepers. The book revealed his love of trees – Shaw mourning the loss of an elm and an ash that grew too near to the house and had to be removed, and celebrating his 'half-grown cedar' as well as his copper beech and mulberry trees.

Ted Hughes at Lumb Bank

Lumb Bank is an eighteenth-century, mill owner's house on the steep-sided clough of the Colden Water. The water rushes along in the narrow valley bottom, to meet the Hebden Water and feed into the Upper Calder river at Hebden Bridge. And it was at Mytholmroyd, just outside Hebden Bridge, that poet and children's author Ted Hughes was born in 1930. The Calder valley in the 1930s, with its working canals, railways and textile mills, would have been a very different place to the one that exists now, with its restored buildings and thriving artistic community. Yet Ted's connection with this place never faltered, despite the fact that his talent catapulted him to a life of fame and travel.

He lived in the Calder valley for just eight years as a boy before the family moved to south Yorkshire, and he once said that those first years shaped everything that came later. He explored this distinctive landscape, which is such a tapestry of contrasts, going shooting with his elder brother and walking the moors. Life was hard for the millworkers down in the valley, and the canals and roads would have been busy with barges and traffic. Above, every available workable piece of land was ploughed or used for hay, sheep or cattle, before the good land gave way to thin, moorland soils.

Ted won an Exhibition to Cambridge, did National Service and began the writing career that would culminate in his being appointed poet laureate. He would not return to the Calder valley for almost twenty years. When he did, it was with his new wife, the American poet Sylvia Plath, to visit his parents, who were now living on Heptonstall Slack. The couple would both write powerful poetry about this Pennine landscape.

'Before these chimneys can flower again
They must fall into the only future, into earth.'

'LUMB CHIMNEYS'

After Sylvia's death in 1963, Ted put their Devon house on the market with a view to buying Lumb Bank. However, the sale fell through, and he remained in Devon with his children. It was six years later, on the day of his mother's funeral in 1969, that he made an offer for Lumb Bank and moved there in the September – although his stay would be for little more than a year.

Ted regularly returned to Devon and was never able to settle at Lumb Bank. His professional life continued to soar, with his first poetry collection receiving the Galbraith prize. In 1970 he married Carol Orchard, and, although they spent a brief time at Lumb Bank in the autumn of that year, by November the house was closed up. Ted and Carol would remain in Devon for the rest of Ted's life.

The story of Ted Hughes and Lumb Bank might have ended there, but it was in Devon that he met John Fairfax and John Moat, who had formed a fledgling organization to support aspiring writers. Ted was an enthusiastic supporter of what became the Arvon Foundation and, in 1974,

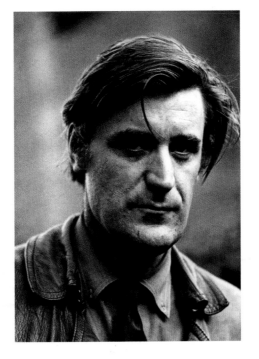

OPPOSITE The view from the garden at Lumb Bank is over the Upper Calder Valley in Yorkshire.
LEFT Fay Godwin, with whom Ted Hughes (1930–98) collaborated on *Remains of Elmet*, took this photo of him in 1971.
FOLLOWING PAGES Lumb Bank was a former mill owner's house, built in the eighteenth century above Colden Water.

ABOVE Lumb Bank is now a centre for creative writing.

RIGHT The fields below the house are used for grazing cattle.

OPPOSITE TOP *Geranium psilostemon* provides a marked contrast to the dark stone of the house.

OPPOSITE CENTRE The Terrace leads through to the Walled Garden at the side of the house.

OPPOSITE BOTTOM The Italian Terrace has been carved into the hillside behind the house and planted with fastigiate yews and box hedging.

he decided to renovate Lumb Bank in order to lease it to Arvon as a northern centre – a place where writers could come and spend a week honing their craft in the company of more experienced authors. The Arvon Foundation took over Lumb Bank in 1975.

As a way of raising money, Ted came up with the idea of the Arvon International Poetry Competition, and in 1980, along with Seamus Heaney and Charles Causley, read every one of the 30,000 entries. The winner was Andrew Motion, who went on to succeed Ted as poet laureate. Carol Hughes was also a big supporter of Arvon and took up the Chair of the Arvon Foundation in 1986.

A Garden Shaped by the Landscape

Lumb Bank is the product of its topography – carved into the north side of the valley and reached by a steep track. It was built from carboniferous gritstone – known locally as millstone grit. This is a hard stone, blackened by soot and weathering, and was used for the house, the terraces and the drystone walls, which criss-cross the fields below. Lumb Bank comprises 8.5 hectares / 20 acres, which slope down to the Colden Water – the woodland in the valley now almost obscuring the old mill chimneys.

The original, eighteenth-century mill owner of Lumb Bank was prosperous and clearly had ideas of grandeur. An Italianate terrace juts out from the rock above the house, complete with niches and bee boles and a pair of fastigiate yews. In front of the house, a narrow terrace has been planted with a perennial border, while the forbidding stone of the house is softened by climbers and clumps of *Geranium psilostemon*. A brick arch links this terrace to the Walled Garden – its sloping aspect to the south suggests it was probably the site of the original Kitchen Garden; it is now used to grow vegetables. Below, a massive, solid wall holds back the earth and a third terrace has been formed, curving out with a ha-ha to keep the cattle at bay. From every aspect, there are views of the valley, known as the Golden Clough, and of the wooded hillside with its tall chimneys – a ghostly reminder of its industrial past. And ever present is the sound of the Colden Water as it hurries on, as if to do business down in Hebden Bridge.

Today, the gardens and wild landscape around Lumb Bank are more than just a backdrop to spending a creative week in the

THE WRITER'S GARDEN

country. They are an integral part of it, as Ted demonstrated in his collaboration with landscape photographer Fay Godwin on the book *Remains of Elmet* – Elmet being a Celtic kingdom that stretched across this moorland landscape. In this book, Ted traced his steps through poems to places that are still on the map today, from 'Lumb Chimneys' to 'Hardcastle Crags', and from 'Widdop' to 'Heptonstall Old Church'. It is both an intensely personal work and a tribute to the industrial past and the people who shaped the Upper Calder valley.

The landscape around Lumb Bank absorbed Ted's mental life and fed his work long after he had left it. The complexity of his life, the restlessness and the tragedies that beset him meant that Lumb Bank never became his permanent home. However, its particular atmosphere is one that has inspired – and will continue to inspire – a new generation of writers.

Written in Residence

LUMB BANK, 1969–70

Ted Hughes was poet laureate from 1984 until his death in 1998. He published poetry collections as well as edited anthologies and also wrote for children.

SELECTED WORKS

The Hawk in the Rain (1957)

Lupercal (1960)

Crow (1970)

Remains of Elmet (1979; photographs by Fay Godwin)

Moortown Diary (1979)

River (1983)

Birthday Letters (1998)

FOR CHILDREN

The Earth-Owl and Other Moon People (1960)

How the Whale Became and Other Stories (1963)

The Iron Man (1968; illustrated by Andrew Davidson)

Photograph of Ted Hughes and his diaries

Henry James *followed by* E.F. Benson at Lamb House

It is perhaps not surprising to find a house and garden that have been loved and lived in by more than one writer. Lamb House, in the Sussex coastal town of Rye, was the home of Henry James, the transatlantic literary genius and author of *The Portrait of a Lady*, who discovered his 'indispensable retreat' in the summer of 1897 and lived there until his death, in 1916. He was followed, in 1919, by E.F. 'Fred' Benson (the man behind the popular humorous Mapp and Lucia novels), who lived at Lamb House until 1940.

The Master

Henry James was fifty-five when he came to Rye. Born in New York, he had studied and travelled in Europe, but had been settled in England for twenty years. His work had marked him out as a brilliant chronicler of what happens when European and American cultures collide, and he had led a cultured life in London. He already knew the Cinque Port town of Rye, perched high above its harbour and the shingle flats that stretch to the English Channel, because he had rented the vicarage there for summer holidays. But when he discovered a red-brick, Georgian house, with a Walled Garden, he was smitten. He stood in the street and made 'sheep's eyes' at Lamb House (named after the family who built it), but feared it would never be his. Fate, it seemed, was on his side. When the owner died suddenly, James was able to lease Lamb House, and then buy it outright in 1899. He loved it immediately, and it appeared as Mr Longdon's home in his next novel, *The Awkward Age*.

Lamb House fulfilled all James's wishes for a refuge from his life in London, where he had been hurt by the critical failure of one of his plays in the city's notoriously savage theatre world. He intended to live at Lamb House from May to October. Although he loved the house, it was in fact the Garden Room (now gone) that first attracted James. He had seen a watercolour by his friend the architect Edward Warren of a

'Old square, red-roofed, well assured of its right to the place it took up in the world . . .'

HENRY JAMES,
THE AWKWARD AGE

Henry James fell hopelessly in love with the Walled Garden of Lamb House in Rye, Sussex.

THE WRITER'S GARDEN

HENRY JAMES AND E.F. BENSON AT LAMB HOUSE

'. . . between the church and her strategic window was the cottage in which her gardener lived, and she could thus see, when not otherwise engaged, whether he went home before twelve, or failed to get back to her garden by one.'

E.F. BENSON, *MISS MAPP*

red-brick edifice built into the garden wall, its bay window leaning out over the street and a little green garden door beneath. This room became James's writing room, and here he would work every morning, walking up and down dictating to his secretary (due to rheumatism he could not write longhand any more). He called the room 'The Literary Muse', and so it proved. From Lamb House, he produced three of his greatest novels: *The Wings of the Dove*, *The Ambassadors* and *The Golden Bowl*. During that period, a circle of friends had settled nearby in the Sussex countryside,

THE WRITER'S GARDEN

including H.G. Wells, Joseph Conrad and Rudyard Kipling, and to this group, as to the wider world, James became known as 'The Master'.

With regards to the garden, however, 'The Master' knew his limitations. In 1898, just after acquiring Lamb House, he admitted that he could hardly tell a dahlia from a mignonette, and he immediately sought the advice of artist and garden designer Alfred Parsons. He proposed a new sweeping lawn area in the garden, which was just over 0.4 hectare/1 acre, with flourishing espaliers

OPPOSITE LEFT Lamb House stands at the end of a narrow, cobbled street and features in both James's and Benson's novels.
OPPOSITE RIGHT St Mary's Church is at the other end of the street in which Lamb House is situated.
BELOW The garden at Lamb House has a mulberry tree, a replacement for the one that was lost in James's lifetime.

around its walls – figs, plums, apricots and pears. Parsons also suggested box-edged borders containing bright flowers – tulips, fuchsias and lupins – a layout that remains very much unchanged to this day, even if the planting has inevitably changed. The mulberry and walnut trees that Parsons recommended have since come down in gales. James was devastated by the loss of the mulberry, which he thought was the embodiment of the garden. A replacement mulberry, planted in the 1950s, still stands.

James appointed a gardener, George Gammon, to whom he was glad to leave all the work. Gammon won prizes at local shows with his vegetables and flowers, which James, very much the Anglophile, was delighted with. The last plant to have a direct association with James was a *Campsis radicans*, which died in 2011, more than a century after it was planted.

Fact into Fiction

Lamb House garden is also the sunny and uplifting setting for one of the great comic masterpieces of the English language – the Mapp and Lucia novels. Set in the 1930s, when the writer E.F. Benson was living at Lamb House, these novels are about Mrs 'Lucia' Lucas and Miss Elizabeth Mapp, rival queens of their little English domains – respectively Riseholme (a fictional village in the Cotswolds) and Tilling (based on Rye).

Benson first visited Lamb House in 1900, with his elder brother Arthur (A.C. Benson), the academic who is probably most famous for penning the words of 'Land of Hope and Glory' – Britain's unofficial national anthem. The younger Benson met Henry James and greatly admired his fiction; it was certainly a factor in Benson taking over the lease of Lamb House in 1919, three years after James's death. Benson shared the house with his brother from 1922, until the latter's death in 1925.

Although Benson always kept a home in Knightsbridge, the summers he spent in Rye signalled a new phase in his writing. He envisaged the fictional Miss Mapp sitting behind the curtains of the Garden Room, spying on all the comings and goings of the town. Her home, Mallards, is Lamb House, and the characters all firmly located in real houses and frequenting shops and inns that can easily be identified today.

The Garden Room, which had been the 'muse' for Henry James, also inspired Benson. When he introduced the monstrous Elizabeth Mapp to his readers, he wrote in the preface: 'I lingered at the window of the Garden Room from which Miss Mapp so often and so ominously looked forth. To the left was the front of her house, straight ahead the steep cobbled way . . . to the right the crooked chimney and the church.'

Benson wrote six wickedly funny Mapp and Lucia novels from Lamb House. The Garden Room, looking over both the garden and the town, would have been the perfect place for observation, but Benson also made himself a secret area outside the main Walled Garden, where he sat at a small table with his notepad, in what he called his 'outdoor sitting room'. The reason Benson retreated to this private space was that his gardener, Gabriel, terrified him, and Benson said that he always felt like a guest in Gabriel's presence, such was the latter's fervour for the garden. This area is not part of the garden any more nor, sadly, is the Garden Room, which was hit by a bomb in 1940.

A Ghostly Past

Benson, like James, never married and lived alone. He loved to take long walks – as James had done before him – down to the shingle flats around Rye harbour. Despite being a sharp observer of the people of Rye, Benson was appointed the town's mayor three times between 1934 and 1937 and was clearly a pillar of the community, even welcoming Queen Mary to the house in 1935 (after having taken her on a whistle-stop tour of the antique shops).

OPPOSITE TOP Henry James took advice from landscape designer Alfred Parsons on the design of the garden.
OPPOSITE CENTRE Japanese anemones flower in the borders at Lamb House.
OPPOSITE BOTTOM Shasta daisies flourish in the Walled Garden.
ABOVE LEFT Henry James (1843–1916) enjoyed relaxing in the garden at Lamb House.
ABOVE CENTRE The Garden Room was used by both James and Benson for writing.
ABOVE RIGHT E.F. 'Fred' Benson (1867–1940) eventually became mayor of Rye.

RIGHT The coastal town of Rye was the model for the fictional village of Tilling in Benson's Mapp and Lucia novels.

RIGHT BELOW Both Henry James and, later, E.F. Benson loved to walk and observe nature on the shingle flats near Rye harbour.

THE WRITER'S GARDEN

Henry James and Fred Benson had two other things in common – their love of dogs and their penchant for writing ghost stories. The dogs are buried in a little pet graveyard in a dark, dank corner of the Walled Garden, perhaps the only corner of Lamb House that gives a clue as to how such a solid, even cheerful house could have been home to the writers of two chilling tales: James's *The Turn of the Screw* and Benson's *The Bus Conductor*. That will remain the true mystery.

Artistic Traditions

Lamb House was given to the National Trust by the widow of Henry James's nephew, and since then has had a succession of literary and artistic tenants including the biographer H. Montgomery Hyde, Rumer Godden (author of *Black Narcissus*) and Sir Brian Batsford (artist and designer of Batsford travel books). In 2009, actress Francesca Rowan co-founded The Lamb Players, who give annual theatre performances in the gardens, and so the literary traditions continue.

Although open to the public, Lamb House remains a family home, and the garden is tended by the live-in tenants. Gradually, more vegetables and espalier fruit are being introduced to reflect the garden's history. The walls are clothed with sweet-smelling jasmine and roses, and in high summer the borders billow with shasta daisies (*Leucanthemum* x *superbum*), fennel, orange daylilies, Japanese anemones and hydrangeas – a contemporary garden that nonetheless reflects the spirit of its previous writers in residence.

Written in Residence

HENRY JAMES, 1898–1916

James, who was born in New York in 1843, became a British citizen in 1915 while living at Lamb House. As well as novels, he wrote dozens of short stories.

The Turn of the Screw (1898)

The Awkward Age (1899)

The Wings of the Dove (1902)

The Ambassadors (1903)

The Golden Bowl (1904)

The Outcry (1911)

The Ivory Tower (published posthumously 1917)

E.F. 'FRED' BENSON, 1919–40

Benson was mayor of Rye in the 1930s and is buried in St Mary's churchyard near Lamb House. He wrote the Mapp and Lucia series of novels, as well as ghost stories.

NOVELS

Queen Lucia (1920)

Miss Mapp (1922)

Lucia in London (1927)

Mapp and Lucia (1931)

Lucia's Progress (UK 1935;

published as *The Worshipful Lucia* in USA)

Trouble for Lucia (1939)

GHOST STORIES

Visible & Invisible (1923)

Spook Stories (1928)

The Bus Conductor (1906;

a short story adapted into the film *Dead of Night* 1945)

John Clare at Helpston

In late summer on Emmonsale's Heath, the young John Clare's mind was probably not on the livestock he was minding. While lying on a patch of sheep-nibbled grass, he would listen to grasshoppers, and let his eyes follow a butterfly as it skipped from grass to grass, or watch the small bees working the wild mint in the damper hollows. When looking up, a circle of clouds might ring his vision, dizzying him and filling his head with words.

Clare, the 'peasant poet' as he became known in literary circles, was born in his parents' rented cottage in the village of Helpston, in 1793. As he grew up, 'botanizing' and poetry were his chief pursuits, and he spent his free time wandering through the fields, woods and heath around his Northamptonshire home. But it was labouring that supported the family, and, as Clare grew into a man, ditch digging, fencing and, largely, gardening were his main jobs. Of all the writers in this book, only Clare was a gardener by trade, and he knew flowers as well as he knew his own name.

Clare the Gardener

Aged fourteen, Clare was taken by his father to meet the master gardener at nearby Burghley House, who was looking for a gardening apprentice. He liked the young man and took him on to work in the kitchen gardens at a wage of eight shillings a week. With this money, Clare not only bought his first work of poetry – James Thomson's *The Seasons* – but also a copy of *Abercrombie's Practical Gardener*, the gardening manual of the day.

As a Kitchen Garden apprentice, Clare's main job would be to take baskets of fruit and vegetables up to the big house. He seems to have done well, although he could not help noticing which wild flowers had self-sown in the vegetable plots, rather than just pulling them out. After his apprenticeship, he worked in the nursery, raising new plants

RIGHT John Clare's birthplace was in Helpston, Northamptonshire.
OPPOSITE The thatched cottage was home to several families when John Clare lived there.

'The wild rose scents the summer air,
And woodbines weave in bowers,
To glad the swain sojourning there,
And maidens gathering flowers.'

'EMMONSALE'S HEATH'

and trees for the estate, earning twelve shillings a week – a far better wage than that of a field labourer. The 1809 Act for the Enclosure of Helpston brought great changes to his village, as previously open fields became divided up. Making a living had always been a struggle for his family, but now, in the new, straitened times, they could afford to rent only two rooms of the cottage, rather than four.

In 1817 Clare left Burghley to take up the more lucrative work of lime-burning in Stamford, and it was here that he met his future wife, Patty, and in 1820 brought her back to live with the

Written in Residence

THE COTTAGE, HELPSTON, 1793–1832

John Clare lived for almost forty years in Helpston,
but spent the latter part of his life in asylums.

Poems, Descriptive of Rural Life and Scenery (1820)

The Village Minstrel, and Other Poems (1821)

The Shepherd's Calendar,

with Village Stories, and Other Poems (1827)

The Rural Muse (published in 1835, after Clare's move
to Northborough)

The statue of John Clare (1793–1864) outside the restored cottage

family in Helpston. At one point, the two rooms the family rented housed John, Patty, his parents, John's sister and a growing band of children. When the number of rooms had been reduced, so had the size of the garden, making it more and more difficult to eke out an existence. Luckily, Clare's father, as the oldest tenant, was able to choose which strip to keep, and he cannily selected the part with the golden russet tree, from which they could at least sell an annual crop of apples.

The Trials of a Poet

Clare had begun composing poems as soon as he could write, but had hidden them from his family, sometimes in a nook above the fireplace, which his mother plundered for papers with which to light the fire. By 1820, now aged twenty-seven, after publication of *Poems, Descriptive of Rural Life and Scenery*, Clare was beginning to be recognized in the wider world. Despite his hatred of enclosure and his defence of agricultural rights, he was sponsored by two landed benefactors: the young Marquess of Exeter, who lived at Burghley, where he had worked, and the Fitzwilliams of Milton Hall, whose estate surrounded Helpston, and where he spent a lot of time with Joseph Henderson, the head gardener.

Henderson became a crucial friend for Clare – bridging the gap between his fellow labourers and the literary community he was starting to mix with. They would go on botany and birdwatching outings together, looking for ferns and orchids, identifying butterflies and swapping seeds to try in their gardens.

Clare's reputation was growing, and he published two more collections of poetry – *The Village Minstrel* and *The Shepherd's Calendar*. Yet, despite his fame, the sales were never enough to feed his growing band of children and his aged parents. He continued to do manual labour, such as hedge cutting and harvesting, despite being one of London's most sought-after literary figures. He suffered with health problems, drank a good deal, and over the coming years would develop depression and worsening mental illness.

Yet it was Clare's love of flowers and nature that continued to fire his writing. When not forced to labour on someone else's land, he would tend the garden at the cottage, particularly after his father became too old to do so. Friends from London sent him gifts of polyanthus, Brompton stocks and hardy geranium seeds, and he often transplanted flowers from the woods. He also started work on a natural history of Helpston, which he would never publish.

He was, in essence, a wildlife gardener. He studied wild flowers with a botanist's eye but a poet's soul. Clare not only witnessed the destruction of habitats intellectually, but he also felt it emotionally. He recorded all the places where wild orchids used to be found in his neighbourhood, 'now all under the plough'. And he could never keep the wild things he loved out of his poetry.

Leaving Home

The garden plot at Helpston still has the same footprint as it had in the late eighteenth and early nineteenth centuries – a rectangle coming off the back of the cottage, and an extra piece of land to the side. It would have been mainly productive with potatoes, onions and herbs for the pot, as well as a few flowers. Yet it was never a big enough garden to support a family – and Clare yearned to be self-sufficient. The Fitzwilliams at Milton Hall came to his rescue, offering him an estate cottage in Northborough, a little way from Helpston with 0.4 hectare / 1 acre of orchard and garden, a common for two cows, and a meadow for making hay.

On 30 April 1832 John, Patty and their six children walked the 5 kilometres / 3 miles to Northborough, past all the places that evoked so much emotion for Clare. The new cottage was bright and spacious, but it was as if Clare had been sent to the other side of the world. He described his sense of dislocation in the poem 'On Leaving the Cottage of my Birth'. In it he tells of his yearning for the bluebells, the woods and the hedges of Helpston and longs to be back on his old bench in the garden.

He missed the Helpston cottage, the heath and everything that was familiar – in fact, everything that had made him the poet he was. Northborough was on the edge of the Great Fen – a vast, watery landscape so unlike the heaths and meadows and woods he knew.

RIGHT ABOVE Clare's family relied on the garden at Helpston for basic vegetables and a crop of apples to sell.

RIGHT A mirabelle plum tree stands at the end of the path that runs between borders of hollyhocks and cottage garden flowers.

'Grasses that never knew a scythe,
Wave all the summer long;
And wild weed blossoms waken blythe,
That ploughmen never wrong.'

'EMMONSALE'S HEATH'

His friend Henderson gave advice on how the garden should be laid out for the best family use. But cut off from his familiar surroundings, Clare's depressions and mental illness worsened, and he was unable to do much more than grow a few vegetables and sell the apple crop from the orchard. There were glimmers of happiness: he wrote of sitting on a bench, instructing the children how to clip the old yews into topiary; and, although writing little, he did start to collect together his best poems, including 'The Nightingale's Nest' and 'Emmonsale's Heath'. It was published as *The Rural Muse*, and everyone agreed it was his finest work.

The Journey Home

Clare would live at Northborough for just a few years. In 1837 his publisher helped to secure him a place in an asylum in Epping – one of the more forward-thinking institutions of its day. There, he got the rest and regular nutrition he needed and was free to walk in the woods, where he found the countryside to his liking. He thought he would be staying for just a few weeks, but weeks became months, and months became years. Clare was clearly improving, but he still had delusions and was desperately homesick. He was sometimes well enough to do gardening and field work, for which he was paid. One observer of the time thought that most of Clare's mental problems stemmed from poor nutrition and uncertainty about his income.

One of the most poignant episodes in Clare's life began one day in summer 1841, when he set out to walk the 145 kilometres/90 miles home to Northamptonshire. He carried only a pocket notebook of

LEFT Ailsworth Heath, Northamptonshire, is one of just a few fragments of the original heath that John Clare knew as Emmonsale's.

the poems he had been writing in the asylum, and he arrived home, hungry, footsore and weary. Six months later he was admitted to the asylum in Northampton, where he would stay for the rest of his life.

Clare was allowed to walk in the grounds there, but his letters home were full of longing for his old life. He asked his children how the flowers in the garden were getting on and told them how he wished he could come home to go searching for wild flowers in the woods.

Changes to the landscape and to rural people in Clare's lifetime were being mirrored in his own life. The freedom to roam on the heath was curtailed after enclosure – hedges and walls barred the way, and common rights to collect wood and graze livestock were gone. When visited in the asylum as an old man, Clare was still working in the kitchen gardens, just as he had begun his working life. But, once inside, the bars of the windows reminded Clare that he was not – and would never be – free to roam again.

In John Clare's Footsteps

The thatched cottage where Clare was born and lived is now run by the John Clare Trust, and it has been substantially restored. The gardens have been redesigned, and in 2013 a new garden was installed based on the Chelsea gold-medal-winning one 'The Rural Muse' by Adam Frost. The Trust runs a programme of exhibitions, workshops and an annual John Clare festival.

Although the landscape around Helpston has changed massively, there are remnants of the wild places that Clare knew and included in his poems. Langley Bush, Royce Wood (now Rice Wood) and Swordy Well (now Swaddywell) still exist, and the parish of Barnack publishes leaflets of walks around John Clare's favourite places. In Clare's day and on old maps, Helpston was written as Helpstone. The surviving areas of limestone heath are now protected by Natural England. The gardens at Burghley House, where Clare worked, are open to the public.

Ailsworth Heath near Helpston

Thomas Hardy at Hardy's Cottage and Max Gate

'It faces west, and round the back and sides
High beeches, bending, hang a veil of boughs
And sweep against the roof.'

'DOMICILIUM'

The Cottage, Higher Bockhampton was home to three generations of Hardys. This cob-and-brick dwelling, with its wheat-straw-thatched roof was built in 1800 by Thomas's great-grandfather. The family ran a building business from the cottage, and stonemasons, bricklayers and other employees would come to the parlour window to collect their weekly wages.

Thomas Hardy's father was musical, and the young boy grew up in a tradition of joining the church choir and band – playing fiddles and other instruments and singing in a folk tradition very different to the organs and choirs of late Victorian times. His mother loved books and had ambitions for her eldest son, earmarking her younger one, Henry, as the one to join the family firm.

Hardy's Cottage was isolated. The surrounding heath and woodlands made a strong image on the young Hardy, who, when aged sixteen, described it in his poem 'Domicilium'. The parlour at the cottage is identifiable in many of Hardy's works, but particularly in *Under the Greenwood Tree*, with its long beams, stone floor and fireplace with a settle on either side. When Hardy was very small, he might have heard the merrymaking of the musicians practising in

RIGHT Thomas Hardy was born in 1840 in Higher Bockhampton, Dorset. His bedroom was directly above the parlour window.
OPPOSITE The thatched cottage was built by Thomas Hardy's great-grandfather and was home to three generations of the family.

THE WRITER'S GARDEN

the parlour, drinking cider and singing down the fern-lined lanes as they weaved their way home to the scattered houses of Higher and Lower Bockhampton. Above the parlour, from his bedroom-window seat, he could look out across the 0.4 hectare/1 acre of ground to the Orchard and the heath – then a closely grazed common land for livestock – and watch the birds and foxes at night. At his little bedside table he began to write poems.

The plot of land that Hardy looked over would have been a working yard, used to store wood, stone and building materials. But it also had a garden, with roses, lilac and variegated box and wild honeysuckle clambering up the walls. The family kept chickens and grew basic vegetables – potatoes, roots and cabbages – and possibly raised a couple of pigs. There was an orchard of cider apples, which were an essential part of any rural-Dorset family's life. Young Hardy would take 'Bockhampton Sweet' apples from the orchard to his friend, who was the son of a bookseller in Dorchester, and trade them for permission to read the books in the shop.

Family Ties

Hardy's Cottage and its garden at Higher Bockhampton represented a way of life that was already disappearing – a theme Hardy would revisit many times in his writing. In 1862, at the age of twenty-two, he left Dorset for London to work for a firm of architects. He specialized in the restoration of churches, and for the next five years lived in London. Yet he never quite broke the ties of home and returned frequently. In 1867 he accepted a job with an architect in Dorchester – and he began his first novel, *The Poor Man and the Lady*. It was not published, but in the early 1870s, in his little

LEFT The old well in front of the house is now surrounded by pots of pelargoniums and calendulas.

RIGHT TOP The garden is full of simple cottage flowers including red crocosmia and white Shasta daisies (*Leucathemum* x *superbum*)

RIGHT CENTRE When Hardy was a boy, the garden at Higher Bockhampton would have been used to store stone and wood for the family's building business. He himself designed the layout of the paths and beds in later life.

RIGHT BOTTOM Cider apples still grow in the Orchard, and the annual cider-making is a long-standing communal tradition in Dorset.

*'To dwellers in a wood
almost every species of
tree has its voice . . .;
the holly whistles as it
battles with itself;
the ash hisses amid its
quivering; the beech
rustles while its flat
boughs rise and fall.'*

UNDER THE
GREENWOOD TREE

RIGHT AND ABOVE Hardy's birthplace
is surrounded by woodlands of
holly, ash, oak and beech. In his
first published novel, *Under the
Greenwood Tree*, Hardy expressed
his deep feeling for trees.
OPPOSITE One of the first jobs
Hardy did on moving into his later
home, Max Gate, in Dorchester, was
to plant a Woodland Walk around
the perimeter of the garden.

THE WRITER'S GARDEN

bedroom above the cottage parlour, Hardy began work on *Under the Greenwood Tree*, a tale about a band of traditional musicians who are soon to be made redundant by the new-fangled church organ. But it is also a love story – a subject much on young Hardy's mind. In Cornwall, in spring 1870, he had met his wife to be, Emma Gifford, who supported him in his determination to make a success of writing and to give up architecture for good.

Moving On

In autumn 1873, while writing *Far from the Madding Crowd*, Hardy took part in his last cider harvest at Bockhampton. He was thirty-three, but, because both families opposed his marriage to Emma, he was still living at home.

The following year he and Emma married quietly in London and spent the next ten years moving between London and a series of houses around the West Country. They lived at Sturminster Newton, where he wrote *The Return of the Native* – drawing heavily on his knowledge of the natural history of Dorset's heaths. In it, he described a hot, August day in the garden of Mrs Yeobright, which sounds very much like his own childhood garden with its vegetable patch and rhubarb.

Hardy's work was getting progressively darker and taking on more challenging themes, but these were always set against the places he knew so well. The idea of a fictional Wessex based loosely on the ninth- and tenth-century Anglo-Saxon kingdom was forming in Hardy's mind.

Max Gate

Hardy's success grew. He felt he was, at heart, a poet, but knew that by writing novels his income would be more substantial. By 1883 he was living in Dorchester and plotting *The Mayor of Casterbridge*. He wanted to design and build a new house for himself and Emma, and found a site 1.6 kilometres / 1 mile outside town, on a chalk ridge, with its own, pure well water.

The fairly modest, two-up, two-down, red-brick villa he designed was set in 0.6 hectare / 1½ acres of grounds. Hardy planned the garden before he had even built the house, making three garden 'rooms': a lower lawn; a middle lawn, where Emma would give

Written in Residence

In his early career, Thomas Hardy concentrated on poetry – something he would return to later in life. However, he was always better known for his novels, many of which were set in his fictional Wessex.

HARDY'S COTTAGE, 1840–74

Under the Greenwood Tree (1872)

A Pair of Blue Eyes (1873)

Far from the Madding Crowd (1874)

MAX GATE, 1885–1928

The Mayor of Casterbridge (1886)

The Woodlanders (1887)

Jude the Obscure (1895)

The Dynasts (three volumes, 1904–08)

Max Gate painted by John Everett in the 1920s

garden parties; and a kitchen garden. In the 1920s productions of his plays were performed on the lower lawn – as they still are today.

In 1883, when Hardy bought the freehold of Max Gate for £450, it was a very open site and so he set about planting 2,000 Austrian pines around the perimeter. Within this, he laid out a Woodland Walk, planting native yew, laburnum, elder and beech, as well as bay, box, plane trees and laurels, which were all popular choices with late Victorian gardeners.

It was trees that Hardy really cared about. The opening lines of *Under the Greenwood Tree* set out his belief that every species of tree had an identifiable sound – a 'voice'. In *The Woodlanders*, written soon after he moved into Max Gate, Hardy clearly understood the good practice of tree planting, as he described Giles Winterbourne's gentle hands spreading out the roots correctly so that each tree would grow healthily. He had physically helped to plant the trees in his own garden and hated them to be cut or pruned.

Hardy gardened organically, and grey water from the house was recycled to water the vegetables. He designed a system to collect rainwater from the guttering, which stored the water under the house. He loved young vegetables and insisted that all raspberries and strawberries were to be picked with their stalks on, so that guests could hold the stalk when eating them. He adored apples too – his favourites being 'Charles Ross' for eating and 'Lane's Prince Albert' for cooking.

A gardener was employed at Max Gate, and the last one, Berty Stephens, left a record of his time there. It offers an insight into Hardy's sometimes contradictory feelings towards the garden. He wanted to be self-sufficient in vegetables, yet loved wildlife and would have nothing done to harm them. Stephens told the story of a hare visiting the garden for two seasons, until he could no longer

put up with the destruction. Hardy finally agreed to help trap it in a net – only deliberately to let it escape at the last minute.

The gardener worked five days a week and half a day on Saturday. His duties included heavy work such as wood cutting, knife sharpening and boot cleaning as well as garden jobs. His last task on a Saturday would be to sweep the drive, to leave it spotless for Sunday visitors.

Some of Hardy's most moving poetry was written after the death of Emma in 1912. In these poems, he imagines her still moving around the garden, and in 'Everything Comes' he remembers how she felt the house was exposed when they first moved in – and how he had responded by planting trees.

LEFT TOP Hardy had trained as an architect and so had Max Gate built to his own designs.
LEFT CENTRE When first built, Hardy's wife Emma thought the brick house was too exposed, so Hardy planted trees and shrubs in the drive to screen it.
LEFT BOTTOM The Hardys employed a gardener and insisted that all the vegetables were grown organically.
RIGHT At Max Gate, Thomas Hardy (1840–1928) and his second wife Florence had a terrier called Wessex.

In the middle of the morning on a normal day at Max Gate, Hardy would break off from writing upstairs in his study, which overlooked the garden, and come down to give instructions to the gardener about planting or harvesting crops. He then liked to stroll along the Woodland Walk, and look at the ferns, primroses and bluebells in spring, which also grew wild beside the drive and in among the shrubs. Hardy disliked bush or standard roses, but loved wilder plants. In the afternoon, he and his second wife Florence would take tea in the conservatory, from where he could watch the birds. The conservatory at Max Gate was always filled with pelargoniums, cyclamen, cinerarias, schizanthus and chrysanthemums.

Return to Childhood

When Hardy's family finally moved out of the old cottage on the edge of the heath at Higher Bockhampton, in 1912, it was let to tenants, one of whom, Herman Lee, worked with Hardy to lay out the garden as a cottage garden. Hardy and Lee set out the beds as we see them today, using the old roofing tiles and stone slates that littered the garden, to edge the island beds.

Hardy's Cottage and Max Gate are now looked after by the National Trust. Both gardens are run organically and weeded totally by hand. At Hardy's Cottage, the vegetable bed has been reinstated and is planted with staple crops such as carrots, potatoes and runner beans, which a family of the nineteenth or early twentieth century would have grown. The flowers also reflect those available at the time – calendula, achillea, solidago, tansy, eryngium, nepeta, asters – and there are also herbs such as marjoram and thyme.

The Orchard has been replanted with old varieties of greengage, damson, plum and medlar. There are also plans to trace and reintroduce some of the local cider apples Hardy wrote about in *Under the Greenwood Tree*: 'Sansoms', 'Stubbards' and 'Five-corners'.

Hardy loved honeysuckle and the native *Lonicera periclymenum* still climbs over the front door and borders of *Crocosmia* × *crocosmiiflora*, which has naturalized in Dorset and other western counties of the British Isles, line the path to the gate.

Even in his first poem, 'Domicilium', Hardy was tapping into the history of his birthplace and his roots, and it is his grandmother's memories of the cottage on the heath that make up the last verse.

In her time, the location was much wilder, the house standing quite alone and not protected by trees, as it came to be when Hardy was young and as it is now.

In some ways, Hardy's attitude to his two gardens can be seen as a constant striving to return to the simplicity of the landscape and the wildlife he had seen from his bedroom window as a child. He never forgot those days, when, with the voices of his ancestors echoing in his head, he first picked up a pen.

OPPOSITE TOP At Hardy's Cottage, a large area of the garden is given over to growing staple crops including runner beans, potatoes and carrots.

OPPOSITE The path to the gate winds through *Crocosmia* x *crocosmiiflora*, a plant that has naturalized around the western coast of Britain.

OPPOSITE CENTRE The outhouse, or potting shed, was added on to the cottage in the nineteenth century.

OPPOSITE FAR RIGHT This insect 'hotel' is made from tiles, pipes and other materials reclaimed from around the cottage, which was once the centre of the Hardy family's building firm.

THOMAS HARDY AT HARDY'S COTTAGE AND MAX GATE

Robert Burns at Ellisland

I n late summer, the swallows line up on the ridged, slate roofs of Ellisland Farm a few kilometres north of Dumfries. Their stay is always too short, and they are preparing to leave for their winter quarters. So it was for Robert Burns, who came to this remote farm when he was twenty-nine, full of romantic optimism for a new life that would last for just a few short years.

This son of a tenant farmer in Alloway, near Ayr, had until then helped to run the family farm with his brothers at Mossgiel, Mauchline. Although he had attained poetic success with the publication in 1786 of *Poems, Chiefly in the Scottish Dialect* and had been feted in Scotland's capital city of Edinburgh, Burns had decided to settle to a more rural life. Ellisland was to be the first home of his own, and he was full of dreams and hopes of making it pay, to support a family, as his writing had yet to do.

He was already in love with an Ayrshire girl, Jean Armour, who had born him twins. Although her parents were against the marriage, Burns hoped to start a new life with Jean in a landscape that he had discovered on a tour of southern Scotland in 1787. The farm belonged to his friend Patrick Miller of Dalswinton, and although Burns was offered the lease of three farms he settled on Ellisland Farm and its 69 hectares/170 acres beside the river Nith.

Working the Land

It was clearly the setting that drew Burns to Ellisland Farm. He was under no illusions about the state of the land, with its stony, badly drained, worn-out soil, and he used this knowledge to reduce the rent to £50 per annum.

Robert and Jean finally married in May 1788, and shortly afterwards he composed 'Of a' the Airts the Wind Can Blaw' for 'my Jean'. By then she was pregnant again, and as the land had no farmhouse Burns's priority was to get a home built for his new wife and family. The building work took ten months. Jean meanwhile remained in Mauchline, and Burns travelled the 74 kilometres/ 46 miles there frequently, on horseback. He was full of plans for

'I have been a farmer since Whitsunday, and am now building a house – not a palace . . . but a plain, simple Domicile for Humility and Contentment.'

ROBERT BURNS, 1788

At the age of twenty-nine, Robert Burns set up home at Ellisland Farm, near Dumfries, with his wife, Jean – the 'bonie lassie' of his poem.

Written in Residence

ELLISLAND, 1788–91

Robert Burns collected tunes and transcribed the words from memory or created his own. He is estimated to have written 130 songs and poems during his time at Ellisland Farm, including 'Auld Lang Syne' – a reworking of a traditional song. He collaborated with publisher James Johnson on a six-volume collection of songs, published as *The Scots Musical Museum* (1787–1803).

'The Wounded Hare' (1789)

'Thou Lingering Star' (1789)

'The Gard'ner wi' His Paidle' (1789)

'The Whistle – A Ballad' (1789)

'Tam O' Shanter: A Tale' (1791)

An engraved version of Alexander Naismyth's 1787 portrait of Robert Burns (1759–1796)

their farm, which had an orchard and a vegetable garden, as well as fields cultivated under the run-rig system – open fields ploughed into long furrows with run-offs in between. On 14 October 1788 he wrote to Jean that the apple crop was sold, and to say how happy he was about her coming to live at Ellisland Farm.

In spring 1789 Jean moved there, bringing with her their only surviving child, Robert, or Bobbie. As was the custom, Robert 'christened' the house by sending in a servant first, holding the family Bible and a bowl of salt for good luck, and following behind with Jean on his arm. In August Jean gave birth to a son, Francis Wallace.

Burns was a knowledgeable farmer and worked the land alongside the hired help, sowing the corn and ploughing. Jean took responsibility for the twelve cows and made butter and cheese. Burns had five horses altogether, used for ploughing, harrowing and one for riding. For feeding the family, there were hens, pigs and a plot of kale and potatoes.

The Ploughman-Poet

Burns was a farmer by day, but a poet by night. He often composed in his head while riding and walking and wrote down the words from memory in the evenings in the parlour, with the children playing around him. The landscape, and particularly the path beside the river Nith, inspired Burns to write some of his best work. It is estimated that he produced a quarter of his literary output in his short three-year stay at Ellisland Farm – 130 songs and poems and more than 200 letters.

It would be far-fetched to call Burns a gardener, as it was probably Jean or one of the helpers who dug the vegetable plot and grew a

OPPOSITE TOP Burns came from a farming family, and when he had the chance to run his own farm he chose Ellisland Farm.

OPPOSITE Burns would spend the evenings writing down the poems and songs he had been composing in his head while out at work during the day. It was in his farmhouse at Ellisland that he reworked an old traditional Scottish song, known as 'Auld Lang Syne'.

OPPOSITE CENTRE The Orchard provided a significant part of the farm's income.

OPPOSITE RIGHT The land at Ellisland Farm was poor, but Burns was a knowledgeable farmer, who raised cattle and crops while his wife Jean tended to the dairy production and poultry.

few flowers for the table. He did, however, understand country life from first-hand experience, and gardening was part and parcel of that life. It was at Ellisland that he composed 'The Gard'ner wi' His Paidle' (spade) in which he shows his emotion for those who worked the land.

The Tam O' Shanter Walk

The poem that Burns considered one of his finest is 'Tam O' Shanter: A Tale', composed while walking along the banks of the river Nith at Ellisland. Burns had become friends with Captain Robert Riddell, the owner of a mansion, just upstream from the farm, called Friars' Carse. It was at Friars' Carse that Burns met Francis Grose, who was compiling *The Antiquities of Scotland*. In memory of his father, Burns asked Grose to include an illustration of the old Alloway Kirk, where William Burns was buried. Grose agreed on the condition that Burns would write a 'witch story' to accompany the drawing. Reputedly, Burns strode up and down the grassy path at Ellisland – now known as Tam O' Shanter Walk – and by the end of the day had the atmospheric, rattling tale of a woman's revenge firmly in his mind.

The Hermitage

Burns would regularly walk across the fields to the parkland and grounds of Friars' Carse, which backed on to his own land. Riddell gave Burns free use of a little stone hermitage in the woods in which to write, and it was there that Burns would reflect and compose lines that are still haunting, two centuries later.

But as Burns was also a notorious lover he used the hermitage to meet Maria Banks Riddell, the sister-in-law of his friend. It served him well as a secret trysting place before walking back over the fields through the avenue of beeches to Jean and his 'bairns'.

OPPOSITE TOP LEFT Friars' Carse was the home of Burns's friend Robert Riddell, who allowed him to use the hermitage as a quiet place to write.
OPPOSITE TOP RIGHT AND OPPOSITE Burns composed one of his most famous ballads, 'Tam O' Shanter: A Tale', walking along the banks of the river Nith at Ellisland Farm.
RIGHT The Hermitage was a folly in the gardens of Friars' Carse. Here Burns wrote several of his most famous poems.

'Grave these maxims on thy soul.
Life is but a day at most,
Sprung from night, in darkness lost:
Hope not sunshine every hour,
Fear not clouds will always lour.'

'VERSES IN FRIARS' CARSE HERMITAGE'

Another result of Burns's association with Riddell and his friends at Friars' Carse was 'The Whistle – A Ballad', written by Burns after observing a drinking contest at the house on 16 October 1789. It is perhaps fitting that Friars' Carse today is a country-house hotel.

The End of Dreams

Meanwhile, Ellisland Farm was struggling, not through lack of care or know-how, but because the land was poor and yields were low. Burns had trained as an Excise man and now pleaded with the local commissioner to give him a job. He took on ten parishes around Dumfries, riding 48–64 kilometres / 30–40 miles a day to visit farms, howffs (pubs) and other businesses to assess their profits and the tax owed. He struggled to write, do the manual labour on the farm, and to hold down the Excise job, which bought him a good income.

Jean remembered Burns wandering out into the barnyard where she found him stretched out on a pile of straw gazing at the stars. He came into the parlour, went to his desk and wrote 'Thou Lingering Star' – what she called 'To Mary in Heaven'. And in that same room he wrote down and reworked the traditional songs that he had collected on his travels. In December 1788, one in particular took his ear, from an old man singing an even older tune, which became 'Auld Lang Syne'.

By autumn 1791 Burns, like the swallows, had decided to fly. The farm was sapping his strength, and he called Ellisland Farm a

'ruinous affair' – a sad end to the hopes and romantic notions he had started with. He, Jean and their children moved to the town of Dumfries, initially into a flat and then into a relatively spacious house. Burns had swapped the beauty of Nitherdale for a life better suited to him physically.

Yet his literary star was not quite extinguished. Before his death at the age of thirty-seven, he would write 'My Love is Like a Red Red Rose' and more than sixty songs, including one of the last things he penned – 'A Man's a Man for A' That'.

During his last illness, Burns was taken to bathe in the Solway Firth, as the doctors hoped that, by immersing his body fully in seawater, a cure would be effected. Jean lived on in the Dumfries house for another thirty-eight years, caring for their children and carrying the memory of her wayward, but brilliant husband.

In his last days, Robert Burns was taken to bathe in the Solway Firth, in the hope of restoring his health.

The Burns Heritage

Ellisland Farm today is cared for by the Friends of Ellisland, a small band of dedicated people who try to keep Burns's time here alive and celebrate the creative work that resulted from its very special setting on the banks of the river Nith. The vegetable garden is no longer cultivated, but there is a small orchard and outbuildings containing old farm equipment. And there are walks: the Tam O' Shanter Walk, near the house; the South Walk by the river Nith; and the Hermitage Walk, which leads across the fields to the grounds of Friars' Carse, where the hermitage in which Burns wrote still stands in the woods. In the town of Dumfries, the house in which Burns lived for the last years of life can be also be visited.

The cottage where Robert Burns was born and lived to the age of seven is in Alloway, Ayrshire and is cared for by the National Trust for Scotland. Burns lived on a succession of tenanted farms in Ayrshire, including Mossgiel, where he was joint tenant with his brother Gilbert, before moving to Ellisland Farm.

Burns's short life and his poetry are celebrated every year on the anniversary of his birthday, 25 January. It is an occasion that brings together people from all over the world for Burns's Night and Burns's suppers. His poems and songs express a yearning for places and people who cannot be together. For many Scottish people – particularly those who have moved away – his poems make a direct connection with their homeland.

THE WRITER'S GARDEN

William Wordsworth at Cockermouth and Grasmere

The story of the poet William Wordsworth begins in the town of Cockermouth, in the north of Cumbria, in the year 1770. Here he was born, the second eldest of five children, in what was the grandest house in the town, with gardens that backed on to the river Derwent and with views to the surrounding hills.

His father was an attorney and agent for the powerful Lowther family, and their house came with the job. At first, young Wordsworth led a charmed life. He was allowed to roam freely – swimming in the river, going on fishing expeditions with his brothers, wandering the countryside with his sister Dorothy and spending halcyon days – lost in a book – while sitting beside the river, which ran just beyond the garden wall. Life there was bountiful. There was plenty to eat from the Kitchen Garden, and the family had servants.

Wordsworth was only eight when his mother died. Thereafter, the children were cared for by their grandparents and various sets of uncles and aunts. William was sent to school in Hawkshead, and Dorothy went to live with a family in Halifax. The children would not be reunited for many years. When Wordsworth was thirteen, his father also died, and a dispute with his father's employer, Sir James Lowther, resulted in poverty and a loss of status for his children, as well as the loss of their childhood home.

The separation from his siblings and the deaths of his parents had a big impact on Wordsworth's poetry. Some of his best poems – in particular, 'The Sparrow's Nest' and 'To a Butterfly' – were the ones looking back to this idyllic childhood in Cockermouth. In the latter poem, Dorothy became Emmeline, 'the historian of my infancy'. In later years, Dorothy described a trip back to their first home. She remembered the Terrace bordering the river Derwent, which had become sadly overgrown. The lovely roses and privet hedge of her childhood had grown so large that the old Terrace had all but disappeared.

'Behind my Father's House he pass'd, close by, Along the margin of our Terrace Walk. He was a Playmate whom we dearly lov'd.'

THE PRELUDE

The river Derwent flows past the Terrace of the house where William Wordsworth was born, in 1770, in Cockermouth, Cumbria.

Rescue Mission

In 1937 the house in which Wordsworth had been born was almost demolished to make way for a bus station. Fortunately, with just a couple of days to spare, this was prevented by a group of local people, who managed to raise the £1,625 to buy the Cockermouth house. It was handed over to the National Trust a year later, and the gardens for many years were laid to lawn before a major restoration in 2004.

Archaeological investigations provided some clues as to the previous layout at what had become known as Wordsworth House and Garden, and it was returned to being a productive garden that also needed to look decorative from the house. However, a lot of this restoration work was damaged by a terrible flood that swept through Cockermouth in 2009. Water, travelling at up to 40km/h/25mph, swept away the east wall of the garden and the back wall of the Terrace, which Dorothy Wordsworth had remembered. The rest of the Terrace had to be demolished later, for safety. Because the Terrace had to be completely rebuilt, the head gardener had the opportunity to rethink the planting in the garden and decided to reinstate it with even more authentic Georgian plants, bringing the garden closer to 1770 – the date of Wordsworth's birth.

The beds at Wordsworth House now contain: old roses; medicinal plants such as bistort; herbaceous plants including asphodelines, *Paeonia officinalis* 'Rubra Plena' and woad; flowers for cutting including globe thistles and echinaceas; and heritage vegetables. Apparently, Georgian peas are hard to come by, but there is a dwarf French bean called 'Lazy Housewife', as well as purslane, orach, sorrel, good King Henry, Welsh onions and the oldest varieties of sweet peas – 'Matucana' and 'Painted Lady'.

The garden also grows a good supply of borage, nasturtium, chive, sweet Cicely and sage flowers – all of which would have been collected for the table in the late eighteenth century. Such flowers were eaten fresh, for their delicate, sweet and savoury flavours, and were used to liven up the plain fare of meat, pies and fish.

Around the brick walls of the garden, oak trellising has been constructed according to the guidelines in Phillip Miller's *The Gardeners Dictionary* of 1768. He advised that [12- to 15cm] 5- to 6-inch squares were ideal for plums, apples and pears, and [20- to 23cm] 8- to 9-inch ones for vines, hops, clematis and roses. Elsewhere, there

are split-oak palisades surrounding the hen enclosure and plant supports made from hazel and willow. Throughout, the National Trust gardeners have used only natural materials – jute string, hemp and wooden stakes – to stay true to the materials that would have been available in Wordworth's time. On the garden walls, greengages, bullace, Morello cherries, 'Mirabelle de Nancy' plums, heritage pears and quinces are decoratively labelled using pieces of recycled, local roofing slate.

ABOVE The Walled Garden behind Wordsworth House and Garden in Cockermouth has been recreated as Wordsworth would have known it – a late eighteenth-century, productive garden of flowers, vegetables, wall-trained fruit and apple trees.

OPPOSITE TOP Wordsworth's father was an agent for the Lowther family, and this Georgian house in the centre of Cockermouth came with the job.

OPPOSITE CENTRE AND OPPOSITE BOTTOM William and his sister Dorothy grew up exploring the river and mountain landscape of the Lake District.

OPPOSITE TOP LEFT AND OPPOSITE TOP RIGHT Flowers grown in the Walled Garden at Cockermouth include borage (opposite top left), which was used to decorate food, and echinaceas (opposite top right), which had medicinal properties.
OPPOSITE BELOW LEFT Field roses (*Rosa arvensis*) have been replanted to recreate the privet and rose hedge that William and Dorothy knew on the river terrace.
OPPOSITE BELOW RIGHT 'Keswick Codlin' is an old Lancashire apple.
BELOW In the perennial vegetable bed, old varieties include broad-leaved sorrel, good King Henry and horseradish.
BELOW RIGHT 'Greenup's Pippin' apples are an eighteenth-century variety from the Lake District.

The Terrace was an important feature in both William and Dorothy Wordsworth's childhood realm. It was here that she described privet and roses scrambling together, making a rough hedge, unlike the way we usually see privet grown. The new planting respects this history – the Terrace being lined with white field roses (*Rosa arvensis*) and wild burnet roses (*R. pimpinellifolia*), both of which have interesting hips (orange and black, respectively). At the end stands a rustic summer house, roofed in oak.

THE WRITER'S GARDEN

Dove Cottage (foreground) in the village of Grasmere was the first home that William and his sister Dorothy made together after years of separation.

> 'There was a time when meadow, grove, and stream,
> The earth, and every common sight,
> To me did seem
> Apparell'd in celestial light.'
>
> 'ODE ON INTIMATIONS OF IMMORTALITY
> FROM RECOLLECTIONS OF EARLY CHILDHOOD'

Hidden from view is a smaller Walled Garden, where two old apple trees stand – a 'Keswick Codlin' from Lancashire and the rare cider apple 'Lady's Finger'. In the main garden, two rows of 'Greenup's Pippin', planted in the 1980s, survived the 2009 flood and produce a good crop of big, sharp, juicy cooking apples.

The Wordsworths at Dove Cottage

Dorothy and William Wordsworth, separated so much as children, always talked and dreamed of setting up home together. But there were many things preventing it.

After a spell at Cambridge, William travelled to France and fell in love with Annette Valon, and in 1792 his daughter Caroline was born. He had intended to marry Annette but was forced to leave France because of the revolution. For the next seven years, he travelled – sometimes with Dorothy and often with his fellow poet and friend, Samuel Coleridge – to the West Country and to Germany. But in 1799 William came back to the Lake District, introducing his friend to the mountains, lakes and rivers he had known as a child.

William and Dorothy found a cottage on the shores of Grasmere, for £8 a year. It was not known as Dove Cottage then – it had been an inn called the Dove & Olive Bough, and their address was simply Town End, Grasmere. They were ecstatically happy. Sometimes they were joined by their brother John, and by Coleridge, who moved to nearby Greta Hall (but often stayed with them for weeks).

In 1799, a few days after moving into the cottage, Wordsworth wrote that Dorothy was very pleased with the house and that she had already started to imagine the summer house with a seat they would build at the top of the steep slope. On that slope they planted

THE WRITER'S GARDEN

ferns, bulbs and wild flowers, collected on their walks or given by local people. They created terraces, grew some of the food plants they would have known from the Cockermouth garden – peas, French and runner beans, bistort, turnips and radishes – and planted honeysuckle and roses against the walls.

It was here that Wordsworth became a professional poet, and for many of his followers Dove Cottage represents the wellspring of his creativity. For the first few years his domestic life was cared for by Dorothy, which meant he could devote his time to writing and walking. They chopped wood for the fire, dug the garden and talked and read poetry to each other. At Dove Cottage, Wordsworth wrote some of his best poetry about flowers and nature, and he would begin the poem for which he is most widely known – 'I Wandered Lonely as a Cloud'.

In 1802 William married his childhood friend, Mary Hutchinson. The cottage, although comfortable, was not large enough for a growing family, so in 1808 the Wordsworths – William, Dorothy, Mary and the three children – moved on, to other houses in the area, finally settling at Rydal Mount a few kilometres away, in 1813.

But Dove Cottage will forever be associated with the poet's romantic genius. Here he felt settled and could look back – especially to the time when his impressions and feelings were those of a young boy and to the idyllic childhood that was taken away from him all too soon.

OPPOSITE ABOVE LEFT William and his sister Dorothy Wordsworth moved to Dove Cottage in Grasmere in 1799.
OPPOSITE ABOVE RIGHT The Wordsworths built a summer house at the top of the steep slope behind the cottage.
OPPOSITE BELOW LEFT The garden was tiny, but the siblings were able to plant climbers around the house and grow a few vegetables and flowers.
OPPOSITE BELOW RIGHT When William married Mary Hutchinson and they had children, the cottage became too small for his growing family.

Written in Residence

COCKERMOUTH, 1770–78
William Wordsworth's childhood in Cockermouth inspired many of his later poems including 'The Sparrow's Nest' and 'To a Butterfly'.

GRASMERE, 1799–1808
The Prelude (begun 1798; fourteen volumes, published posthumously 1850)
Poems, in Two Volumes (1807)

The poem 'I Wandered Lonely as a Cloud' was inspired by coming across a swathe of wild daffodils on a walk with Dorothy around Ullswater in April 1802. The poem was published in *Poems, in Two Volumes*. A revised version was published in 1815.

A portrait of William Wordsworth (1770–1850) engraved by John Cochran

Walter Scott at Abbotsford

There were few nineteenth-century writers who did not read Walter Scott. He was the first romantic novelist and the most successful author of his time. Jane Austen, on reading his first novel, *Waverley*, said that, as Scott was already a well-known poet, he had no business to write such good novels.

Like Robert Burns, Scott was a collector of traditional Scottish songs, and by the time he came to Abbotsford at the age of forty he was already wealthy and successful in his careers – firstly as an advocate in the law courts in Edinburgh, and secondly as a poet. His five romantic ballads included *The Lay of the Last Minstrel*, *Marmion* and *The Lady of the Lake*, the last selling 23,000 copies in its first year – unheard of for a work of poetry.

The Perfect Setting

Scott's move from the city of Edinburgh to rural Selkirkshire marked the beginning of a new phase in his literary career – that of novelist. His work as Sheriff-Depute for Selkirkshire brought him often to the border country south of Edinburgh. Here, in 1811, he found a dilapidated farmhouse – then called Cartley Hole. It was set in the most perfect position on a bank of the river Tweed.

He renamed his estate Abbotsford and began the process of altering the house that would devour his earnings, but also bring him great pleasure. Over the next fourteen years Scott would transform the humble farmhouse into a fantastical 'castle'. Even before a brick was laid, Scott was busy planting trees to turn this 'bare haugh and bleak bank' into a wooded Eden. His first priority was to acquire more land, and he increased the original 44 hectares/110 acres

'. . . while my trees grow, and my fountain fills, my purse, in an inverse ratio, sinks to zero'.

WALTER SCOTT, 1812

to 243 hectares/600 acres. He also added a garden wall around the existing vegetable garden, which stood to the east of the house.

The reason that the house and grounds work so well together is that Scott designed the garden at the same time as the house. He was helped by a 'committee of taste', including William Atkinson, James Skene and the actor Daniel Terry, whose wife Elizabeth Terry painted one of the most enduring scenes of Abbotsford.

As his wealth and circumstances grew, Scott started a second phase of development in 1817, converting the farmhouse into a 'cottage ornee', and he had plans for a circular lawn and driveway. By 1822 the now Sir Walter Scott had increased his demesne to 566 hectares/1,400 acres and was busy planting more trees, knocking down the farmhouse and building the baronial house we see today. He built a new Kitchen Garden to the west of the original one (now called the Walled Garden) and the old Kitchen Garden was converted into a sunken court (now the

OPPOSITE Agapanthus flourishes in the Walled Garden at Abbotsford, in the Scottish Borders.
LEFT A portrait of Sir Walter Scott (1771–1832) engraved by James Thomson.
FOLLOWING PAGES The monks from nearby Melrose Abbey used to ford the river Tweed from the land that Scott purchased for this house – hence its name, abbots' ford.

RIGHT Scott created Abbotsford over a period of some fourteen years, spending all his considerable wealth on adding to the house and extending the walled gardens.

RIGHT BELOW Clipped yews were planted in the South Court during the Victorian period.

OPPOSITE TOP Scott's favourite deerhound, Maida, is buried beneath the sculpture just outside the entrance door.

OPPOSITE CENTRE Scott was a great collector of historical artefacts and had Roman panels set into niches around the South Court.

OPPOSITE BELOW The statue that gave its name to the Morris Garden is from Scott's novel *Rob Roy*.

THE WRITER'S GARDEN

Morris Garden) enclosing the entrance court (now South Court) with a stone arcade.

Abbotsford's Garden

Visitors would have arrived at Abbotsford under the imposing, if somewhat tongue-in-cheek, portcullis-style gateway into the South Court. There would have been a turning circle for carriages, as well as lawns and flower borders. The layout today is still recognizably Scott's, although the clipped yews are a Victorian addition. Niches in the south and west walls were designed to hold Scott's collection of Roman panels and other antiquities. Originally, he had a more delicate trellis of greenery around them, but this has developed over time into a dense hedge of yew. The planting in the South Court was flamboyant, perhaps due to the input of Scott's gardener William Bogie, who had come from Dalkeith Palace. According to Scott: 'He has done wonders for me in the garden way' and was responsible for the narrow beds of hollyhocks and roses along the arcade and a leafy, honeysuckle-covered pergola.

On the other side of the arcade is the Morris Garden, so-called because of the statue that Scott commissioned of his own character from *Rob Roy*. Sadly, both the sculptor, John Greenshields, and Scott died before it was finished. Morris is begging forgiveness, but his hands were never completed, giving the figure even more pathos. Because the Morris Garden is enclosed by high walls, it has the feel of a cloister. Scott's plan was for it to be a grassy 'garth' with viewing terraces, although he did create a path right across the middle, for a direct crossing. He added the flag tower in 1824, which may have been used as a fruit store.

The Walled Garden was Scott's most ambitious project for the garden at Abbotsford. He wanted to provide the best fruit and vegetables for his many visitors. It has a typical Regency, south-west orientation and slopes to make the best of the light. This is particularly important in this part of Scotland, where gardeners have to make the most of the long summer days and the low light levels in winter. The layout is as Scott designed it – 0.4 hectare / 1 acre of ground, with paths and box hedging dividing the space into quarters, and double herbaceous borders running up to the conservatory. Like the house, the conservatory had the latest glazing and heating.

THE WRITER'S GARDEN

Receipts dated December 1821 and January 1822 from William Lamb Seed Merchants, Selkirk, confirmed that Scott bought a vast array of vegetable seeds, including Portugal onions, speckled kidney beans, 'Sugarloaf' cabbage, shallots and radishes, as well as hyacinth bulbs. In the twenty-first century the bias has shifted towards flowers, with penstemons, agapanthus, phlomis, alstroemerias, crocosmias, echinaceas and kniphofias dominating the central planting. To one side grow raspberries, strawberries, cabbages and two old apples – 'Scotch Bridget' and 'Tower of Glamis' – names that conjure up Scott's obsession with history. The trees themselves were planted in the early twentieth century.

Scott's French wife, Charlotte, loved cut flowers, and this tradition is also continued in the Walled Garden. Dahlias are the highlight of the late summer display, although they cannot be left out in the tough Scottish winter, which at Abbotsford can mean temperatures staying below –10°C/14°F for several weeks. Scott himself tried unsuccessfully to grow pineapples and peaches, but did better with grapes and melons under glass.

Man of Trees

Nothing gave Scott more pleasure than tree planting on the estate, with Tom Purdie, his estate manager. Purdie had appeared before Scott on a poaching charge, and he became a great friend and employee of Scott's. Together they created the Tweed-side, wooded landscape at Abbotsford. Scott helped to plant the trees and said that he could happily work at pruning and planting from morning until night. Purdie would rap on the panes of Scott's study to tell him that it was time to come out. Scott then would go to the anteroom, open

OPPOSITE ABOVE The Walled Garden at Abbotsford is exactly as Scott designed it, with beds for fruit, flowers and vegetables and a south-facing conservatory.
OPPOSITE BELOW LEFT The stone entrance arch to the Walled Garden is deliberately impressive.
OPPOSITE BELOW RIGHT Phlomis and *Verbena bonariensis* grow in front of the conservatory that Scott had built in 1824.
ABOVE RIGHT The double herbaceous borders run the entire length of the Walled Garden and include alstroemerias, lilies, salvias, phlomis, agapanthus and sedums.
RIGHT Dahlias provide late summer colour in the cut-flower borders.

the windows to check the weather, pull on his coat and set off across the hillside with his dogs.

A Change in Fortune

The extraordinary building of Abbotsford – with its fairytale turrets and storybook interior – had been funded partly against future earnings. The collapse, in 1826, of his Edinburgh publishers, Constable, and his involvement with his printing partner, James Ballantyne, had left Scott fully exposed to the losses. He was, in effect, bankrupt. As bankruptcy meant losing Abbotsford and not paying those he owed, Scott instead asked to be allowed to pay off the debts through his writing. His unusual request was granted, and Abbotsford was placed in a trust. For the rest of his life, every penny he earned from his writing went to make up the shortfall.

Scott wrote in a study on the ground floor. In it was a staircase so that he could slip from his bedroom unseen, often in his nightwear, to start work early in the morning. He wrote fast until lunch – often without including punctuation, using a nib pen and ink, dried with a blotter. His life became one of relentless work. especially after the death of his wife, Charlotte, also in 1826. Thereafter, he was cared for by his daughter Anne and lived to see his granddaughter, Charlotte, who would become one of the women to take the Abbotsford story into the next generations. The bulk of Scott's debts were, in fact, paid back in his lifetime, and the rest settled on his death.

In 1831 he travelled to Europe for the winter, but pined for Abbotsford. He suffered a series of strokes and began to make the long journey home via Germany and London. He knew he had not long to live and wanted to spend those precious days at Abbotsford, to see his gardens, his trees and the view down to the river Tweed.

Scott arrived back in July 1832 and had a camp bed erected in the dining room, from where he could see the river. He wrote about his sheer joy at being back home and died there in September 1832 – with, it is said, a pen in his hand.

Scott missed Abbotsford when he was away, and his dying wish was to return home and look out of the window towards the river Tweed and the hills beyond.

THE WRITER'S GARDEN

Abbotsford after Scott

Abbotsford has always been a showcase house – to be seen and admired. It was opened to the public just a year after Scott's death and was soon attracting visitors from across the world. His granddaughter Charlotte inherited the estate in 1853. With her husband James Hope, she was responsible for putting in the sunken path in the Morris Garden, which led visitors to a side door into the house, thereby keeping the South Court as their private garden.

Women continued to play an important part in protecting Sir Walter Scott's legacy at Abbotsford. His great-grandaughter Mary Monica devoted herself to the estate, a passion she instilled in her son, Major General Sir Walter Maxwell Scott. For the latter half of the twentieth century, his two daughters, Mrs Patricia and Dame Jean Maxwell Scott cared for Abbotsford, completing an unbroken family connection with the great man.

Since 2007 the estate has been solely in the hands of the Abbotsford Trust. The estate includes the house, gardens and stretches of the river Tweed as well as the oak and pine woods that Scott set out in the early nineteenth century. Walks through the estate lead through the trees that Walter Scott planted, never of course living to see them as we do today.

Written in Residence

ABBOTSFORD, 1811–32

Walter Scott began his writing career as a poet, but was probably best known as a novelist, producing twenty-three bestsellers, including the nine *Waverley* novels, as well as works of biography. Some eighty operas and musical works have been based on Scott's work including Rossini's *La Donna del Lago* (*The Lady of the Lake*) and Donnizetti's *Lucia di Lammermoor* (from *The Bride of Lammermoor*). All of Scott's novels were produced from Abbotsford. In 1825, seven years before his death, he began writing a journal of his life there.

Waverley (1814)

The Antiquary (1816)

Rob Roy (1817)

The Heart of Midlothian (1818)

The Bride of Lammermoor (1819)

Ivanhoe (1819)

Kenilworth (1821)

The Talisman (1825)

The Journal of Sir Walter Scott

(written 1825–32, published posthumously)

The monogram of Sir Walter Scott carved in the stone and woodwork at Abbotsford

Rudyard Kipling at Bateman's

One of the most frequently quoted of all gardening poems is probably 'The Glory of the Garden' by Rudyard Kipling. It is a rousing celebration of hard-working gardeners everywhere, and it was written by a man whose skill with his pen gave him the chance to create his own glorious garden in the Sussex countryside.

Bateman's is cocooned within the Dudwell valley – an area of wooded hillsides, fast-flowing streams and rich, clay soil. Rudyard Kipling lived here from 1902 until 1936, and his wife, Carrie, left the house and its entire contents to the National Trust in 1939. For this reason, Bateman's is one of the most complete examples of a writer's home to be found anywhere, and the spirit of the Kiplings still pervades the estate that surrounds it.

Rudyard Kipling's father, John Lockwood Kipling, was an artist and architectural sculptor who went to teach in Bombay and later became the curator of the museum in Lahore. After a spell on the local paper there, young Kipling began writing short stories and was soon the best-known writer about India in the English language. He settled in London in 1889, and in 1892 married an American, Caroline Balestier, known as Carrie.

The couple tried to settle in New England, where they built a house on a 4.4-hectare/11-acre property in Vermont near her family. But in 1897, after a very public row with Carrie's brother, they returned with their children to Britain and settled in Rottingdean on the Sussex coast. All was well until, on a visit to New York in 1899, Kipling and his daughter Josephine contracted pneumonia. Kipling himself almost died, but he recovered, only to learn that Josephine had died, aged six. It was a tragedy from which he and Carrie would never really recover. Their house in

'Our England is a garden,
and such gardens are not made
By singing:- "Oh how beautiful!"
and sitting in the shade.'

'THE GLORY OF THE GARDEN'

RIGHT Bateman's was built in 1634, probably by a local ironmaster. The paths are made from a fossil stone known as Sussex marble.
OPPOSITE Rudyard Kipling and his wife Carrie bought Bateman's in 1902 and began creating a series of gardens around the house.

Rottingdean held too many memories for Kipling. In addition, the success of *The Jungle Books* had catapulted this reserved man into the limelight, and he found such celebrity overwhelming. When he saw Bateman's, he realized that it was the retreat from the outside world that he had been looking for.

In 1902 the Kiplings moved into the house, which was surrounded by 13 hectares/33 acres of gardens, meadows and woods. For his surviving children, John and Elsie, Bateman's became the setting for an idyllic childhood, as they acted out plays in the old quarry and visited the mill by the river – events that would find their way into Kipling's two classic children's stories *Puck of Pook's Hill* and *Rewards and Fairies*.

Earth and Stone

Bateman's was built in 1634, in sandstone, probably by an ironmaster – this part of East Sussex being known for its rich seams of iron ore and plentiful chestnut and hornbeam woods for charcoal. In his autobiography Kipling referred to Bateman's as 'The Very-Own House', and he loved the fact that it seemed to have emerged from the earth – the stones quarried just a few metres from the house and the roof tiles made from the local clay.

Kipling was already incredibly wealthy when he bought Bateman's, and he threw all his energy and finances into it, furnishing the house with seventeenth-century oak furniture, clocks and wall hangings. He also enhanced the garden, planting an orchard, dividing up the

THE WRITER'S GARDEN

spaces with yew hedges and designing a Kitchen Garden within the walls of what is now known as the Mulberry Garden.

Creating a Garden

In 1907 Kipling won the Nobel Prize for Literature, the first British recipient of the honour. It came with prize money of £7,700 – enough for Kipling to start major improvements on the gardens. To the front of the house, he wanted to keep the look clean and simple, so it was laid to lawn, with small shrub borders around the front door. To the side, a previous owner had planted two parallel rows of pleached limes – *Tilia platyphyllos* 'Rubra' – to set the formal tone.

ABOVE LEFT, ABOVE CENTRE AND ABOVE RIGHT Rudyard Kipling planted an orchard and laid out a vegetable garden above the house, in which he grew medlars (above left), kale and runner beans up wigwams (above centre) and 'Conference' pears (above right).
LEFT The Kiplings were looking for a place away from the public and loved this peaceful setting in the Sussex Weald.

Here, Kipling created two different levels: an upper terrace nearest the house, known as the Quarter Deck; and a lower level reached by several sets of wide, stone steps. Because the river Dudwell is tidal, the lower lawn often floods, so Kipling could well have stood on his 'quarter deck' looking over the water.

In the Orchard, Kipling planted a variety of fruit trees including a 'Beauty of Bath' apple, which still stands. Many of the trees were later lost, but the Orchard has been replanted with medlars, pears, mulberries and several different varieties of russet apples.

At the bottom of the sloping Orchard, Kipling also designed and engineered the Pear Allée. This is a long, curved ironwork frame against which have been planted 'Winter Nelis', 'Doyenné du Comice' and other pear varieties. It is aligned with the large ironwork gates bearing Kipling's initials, which lead into the walled Mulberry Garden. This was an old stable yard when the Kiplings arrived, and they converted it into a growing area for fruit and vegetables. This has been reinstated, not as a replica of how the Kiplings had it but as a place to grow ornamentals and

RIGHT Visitors enter the garden between the Orchard and the Herb Border.

RIGHT BELOW The Pear Allée was designed and installed by Kipling. It was replanted in 2000 with old varieties including 'Winter Nelis', 'Doyenné du Comice' and 'Beurré Hardy'.

OPPOSITE LEFT The path leading into the Mulberry Garden is made with local bricks, inset at regular intervals with millstones.

OPPOSITE RIGHT The cut-flower beds in the Mulberry Garden are edged with box and filled with soft grasses and the dramatic *Amaranthus caudatus* 'String of Beads'.

THE WRITER'S GARDEN

some culinary plants in the potager style – as an adjunct to the larger working Kitchen Garden. The borders here are planted with flowers for cutting, and in early autumn the star of the show is amaranthus, growing among soft grasses and other annuals. In the centre, a young black mulberry has been planted to replace the original tree, which Kipling would have known.

The river Dudwell winds its way through the garden and makes up a large part of its character. This tributary, which is just 16 kilometres/10 miles long, rises in nearby Heathfield and makes its way through the Bateman's estate and into the river Rother.

A path through the Wild Garden leads to an old mill, which features in *Puck of Pook's Hill*. Kipling tried very hard to establish whether the mill had been *in situ* since Domesday; however, the building that stands dates from 1750. In spite of his interest in the mill's history, Kipling replaced its mechanism for grinding wheat with one of the first hydroelectric power turbines. This generated

enough electricity for ten light bulbs in the house. (Today, the mill is once again producing flour on a regular basis.)

Kipling also used the mill pond to supply the gravity-fed fountain in the Rose Garden, which links via a small rill to the lily pond. He sketched out a plan, which is framed and still hangs in his upstairs study at Bateman's. It shows the formal pool, Rose Garden and fountain, almost exactly as it looks today. The pond was tranquil enough for water lilies to thrive and, being only a little over 30cm/12in deep, John and Elsie Kipling used it for bathing and had a small boat to get from one side to the other.

The Rose Garden is designed in quarters with the fountain at its centre. It is planted with the original, long-flowering floribunda roses that Kipling chose: *Rosa* 'Betty Prior', *R.* 'Frensham' and *R.* Valentine Heart (a close replacement for the original, pale pink *R.* 'Mrs Inge Paulsen', which is no longer available). Beyond is Kipling's sundial, on which he had carved the words: 'It's later than you think.' A trip around Bateman's often ended at the sundial, where Kipling hoped his guests would take the hint to leave.

A Historical Landscape

Kipling gradually extended his land by purchasing farms as they became available. He acquired 20.5 hectares/51 acres at Rye Green Farm, 6.5 hectares/16 acres at Little Bateman's, for example, until he owned a total of fourteen different properties and had an estate of more than 121 hectares/300 acres. He wanted the land as a protective zone. The woods – or 'shaws' as they are known in this part of Sussex – and any unproductive, small pockets of land were just as important to him as the dairy herds and arable fields. His much-loved poem 'The Way Through the Woods' expressed his desire to dig back into the past, to reveal the layers of history that the landscape held.

Much of Kipling's estate was tenanted, and his ideas about recreating a historical landscape, rather than a purely profitable one, were not popular. When he could, he managed the farms himself, taking advice from the agricultural campaigner and writer H. Rider Haggard, who was a close friend.

Kipling loved children, and, despite losing Josephine, the pre-First World War years at Bateman's were happy ones. The gardens were

OPPOSITE ABOVE Park Mill, which features in Kipling's children's stories, is a working flour mill again.
OPPOSITE BELOW The mill is powered by water from the river Dudwell, which flows through the garden at Bateman's.
LEFT The banks of the Dudwell have been planted with moisture-loving *Gunnera manicata*.

THE WRITER'S GARDEN

designed to be fun, to be played in. Children were always welcome visitors and would be taken out on the pond in a little pleasure boat. Visitors included Kipling's cousin, the political leader Stanley Baldwin, as well as the artists Edward Burne-Jones and Edward Poynter, who had each married one of Kipling's aunts. Yet, like many families, everything was shattered by the outbreak of the First World War, in which John, aged eighteen, volunteered to fight. His death in 1915 at the Battle of Loos completely destroyed his parents, and he is immortalized in the poem 'My Boy Jack'.

To the Future

Life at Bateman's was never quite the same again, and their remaining daughter Elsie eventually left, aged twenty-eight, to marry George Bambridge and live at Wimpole Hall in Cambridgeshire. In 1939 Bateman's passed to the National Trust and is now farmed as one estate, staying true to Kipling's principles of conserving ancient meadows and woods. And, when the autumn sunlight warms the red-brick chimneys and the orchard is laden with fruit, Bateman's still possesses the sense of permanence that must have stirred Kipling to write: 'And the glory of the garden . . . shall never pass away!'

OPPOSITE ABOVE LEFT In the Formal Garden at Bateman's, Kipling chose long-flowering, pink roses including *Rosa* 'Betty Prior'.
OPPOSITE ABOVE RIGHT Kipling had the sundial engraved with the words 'It's later than you think.'
OPPOSITE The Formal Garden was built exactly as Kipling designed it – with a shallow pool, rose beds and yew hedges. The pleached Lime Avenue was planted in 1898, a few years before Kipling bought Bateman's.

Written in Residence

BATEMAN'S, 1902–36

Rudyard Kipling's move to Bateman's marked the beginning of his fascination with the history of England and the particular landscape of the Sussex Weald, with its oaks, chestnuts, streams, valleys, mills, forges and farms. This is the background that pervades his next two books, in which he makes the Roman, Saxon, Norman and medieval worlds exciting for children:

Puck of Pook's Hill (1906)
Rewards and Fairies (1910)

With Dan and Una as the central characters – based closely on his own children John and Elsie – these books are firmly rooted within the Bateman's estate. The Mill (Park Mill), Little Lindens (Rye Green Farm) and Pook's Hill (Perch Hill) are easily identifiable on the ground and on walks around the estate.

Rudyard Kipling (1865–1936)

Garden Visiting Information

Note: All houses and gardens may close on certain days. Check current opening times on their websites.

Jane Austen (pages 10–19)
Godmersham Park, Godmersham, Kent CT4 7DT. Private estate, but the gardens open under the National Gardens Scheme (NGS); www.ngs.org.uk/. The heritage centre holds Jane Austen collections: www.godmershamheritage.webs.com/.
Jane Austen's House Museum, Chawton, Alton, Hampshire GU34 1SD; www.jane-austens-house-museum.org.uk/.
Chawton House Library, Chawton, Alton, Hampshire GU34 1SJ; www.chawtonhouse.org/. Regular guided tours of the house and self-guided tours of the gardens. Public access to the library of early women's writing (1600–1830) by appointment and online.
• Goodnestone Park Gardens, Kent CT3 1PL; www.goodnestoneparkgardens.co.uk/. Belonged to the family of Elizabeth Bridges, the wife of Jane's brother Edward. Jane would have known the 6 hectares/15 acres of gardens.
• Stoneleigh Abbey, Kenilworth, Warwickshire CV8 2LF; www.stoneleighabbey.org/. Owned by Thomas Leigh, a cousin of Mrs Austen. The grounds were designed by Humphry Repton, and Jane visited to see the improvements.
• The Vyne, Vyne Rd, Sherborne St John, Hampshire RG24 9HL; www.nationaltrust.org.uk/vyne/. Owned in the eighteenth century by the Chute family, acquaintances of the Austens when they lived at Steventon in Hampshire.

E.F. Benson *see* **Henry James**

Rupert Brooke (pages 20–7)
The Old Vicarage, Grantchester, Cambridgeshire CB3 9ND. Private house and garden, but the garden occasionally opens for charity.
• The Orchard Tea Garden, 45–47 Mill Way, Grantchester CB3 9ND; www.orchard-grantchester.com/. *The History of the Orchard Grantchester* is available from here and from the adjacent museum (see below).
• The Rupert Brooke Museum, 45–47 Mill Way, Grantchester CB3 9ND; www.rupertbrookemuseum.org.uk/.

Robert Burns (pages 130–37)
Ellisland Farm, Holywood Rd, Auldgirth, Dumfries DG2 0RP; www.ellislandfarm.co.uk. Cottage (guided tours only), grounds and riverside walks.
• Friars Carse Hotel, Auldgirth, Dumfries DG 0SA; www.friarscarse.co.uk/. Grounds, woodland and riverside walks including the hermitage.
• Robert Burns Birthplace Museum, Murdoch's Lone, Alloway, Ayr KA7 4PQ; www.burnsmuseum.org.uk/. National Trust for Scotland cottage, museum and grounds.
• Robert Burns House, Burns Street, Dumfries DG1 2PS; www.dumgal.gov.uk/museums/. Town house where Burns spent his last years.

Agatha Christie (pages 36–43)
Greenway, Greenway Rd, Galmpton, Brixham, Devon TQ5 0ES; www.nationaltrust.org.uk/greenway/. House and gardens.

Winston Churchill (pages 76–83)
Chartwell, Mapleton Rd, Westerham, Kent TN16 1PS; www.nationaltrust.org.uk/chartwell/. House and gardens.

John Clare (pages 114–19)
John Clare Cottage, 12 Woodgate, Helpston, Cambridgeshire PE6 7ED; www.clarecottage.org/. Cottage and gardens.
• Castor Hanglands National Nature Reserve, 6.5 kilometres/4 miles from Peterborough. www.naturalengland.org.uk/.
• Burghley House, Stamford, Lincolnshire PE9 3JY. www.burghley.co.uk/.

Roald Dahl (pages 54–61)
Gipsy House is not open to the public.
• The Roald Dahl Museum and Story Centre, 81–83 High Street, Great Missenden, Buckinghamshire HP16 0AL; www.roalddahlmuseum.org/. Includes a recreation of the interior of Roald Dahl's writing hut.
• Maps and guides to walks in the Chilterns, including the woods that inspired *Danny The Champion of the World*; www.chilternsaonb.org/.

Charles Dickens (pages 62–7)

Gad's Hill Place, Higham, Rochester, Kent ME3 7PA. Guided tours of the house and gardens can be booked via Gravesham Borough Council; www.gogravesham.co.uk/. The house is part of Gad's Hill School; www.gadshill.org/.
• Eastgate House, High Street, Rochester, Kent ME1 1ER; www.medway.gov.uk/. Site of Dickens's Swiss chalet.
• Restoration House, 17–19 Crow Lane, Rochester, Kent ME1 1RF; www.restorationhouse.co.uk/. Gardens and house. Thought to be the inspiration for Miss Havisham's house in *Great Expectations*.

Thomas Hardy (pages 120–29)

Hardy's Cottage, Higher Bockhampton, near Dorchester, Dorset DT2 8QJ; www.nationaltrust.org.uk/hardys-birthplace/. House and gardens.
Max Gate, Alington Ave, Dorchester, Dorset DT1 2AB; www.nationaltrust.org.uk/max-gate/. House and gardens.

Ted Hughes (pages 98–105)

The Ted Hughes Arvon Centre, Lumb Bank, Heptonstall, West Yorkshire HX7 6DF; www.arvonfoundation.org/lumbbank/. Writing centre run by the Arvon Foundation, offering residential creative writing courses; the other regional centres are based in Shropshire, Devon and Scotland.
• The Elmet Trust, based in Ted Hughes's birthplace of Mytholmroyd, near Hebden Bridge, promotes and celebrates the life of the poet with festivals, events and walks; www.theelmettrust.co.uk/.

Henry James and E.F. Benson (pages 106–13)

Lamb House, West Street, Rye, East Sussex TN31 7ES; www.nationaltrust.org.uk/lamb-house/. House and gardens; limited opening days.

Rudyard Kipling (pages 158–67)

Bateman's, Bateman's Lane, Burwash, East Sussex TN19 7DS; www.nationaltrust.org.uk/batemans/. House and gardens.

Beatrix Potter (pages 44–53)

Hill Top, Near Sawrey, Hawkshead, Ambleside, Cumbria LA22 0LF; www.nationaltrust.org.uk/hill-top/. House and gardens.
• Beatrix Potter Gallery, Main Street, Hawkshead LA22 0NS; www.nationaltrust.org.uk/beatrix-potter-gallery/. The solicitor's office of William Heelis houses a collection of original drawings and watercolours from Beatrix Potter's books.

John Ruskin (pages 28–35)

Brantwood, Coniston, Cumbria LA21 8AD; www.brantwood.org.uk/. House, gardens and estate; also exhibitions and courses.

Walter Scott (pages 148–57)

Abbotsford, Melrose, Roxburghshire TD6 9BQ; www.scottsabbotsford.co.uk/. House, gardens and estate.

George Bernard Shaw (pages 92–7)

Shaw's Corner, Ayot St Lawrence, near Welwyn, Hertfordshire AL6 9BX; www.nationaltrust.org.uk/shaws-corner/. House and gardens.

Laurence Sterne (pages 84–91)

Shandy Hall and Gardens, Coxwold, York YO61 4AD; www.laurencesternetrust.org.uk/. House and gardens.

Virginia Woolf (pages 68–75)

Monk's House, Rodmell, Lewes, East Sussex BN7 3HF; www.nationaltrust.org.uk/monks-house/. House and gardens.

William Wordsworth (pages 138–47)

Wordsworth House and Garden, Main Street, Cockermouth, Cumbria CA13 9RX; www.nationaltrust.org.uk/wordsworth-house/. Wordsworth's childhood home. House and gardens.
Dove Cottage, Grasmere, Cumbria LA22 9SH; www.wordsworth.org.uk/. House, garden, museum, poetry readings, talks and events.
• Rydal Mount, Ambleside, Cumbria LA22 9LU; www.rydalmount.co.uk/. Wordsworth's home in later years. House and garden.

OTHER PEOPLE AND PLACES MENTIONED IN THE TEXT

• J.M. Barrie's Birthplace, 9 Brechin Road, Kirriemuir, Angus DD8 4BX; www.nts.org.uk/.
• Great Maytham Hall, Rolvenden, Kent TN17 4NE; www.sunleyheritage.co.uk/. Gardens sometimes open under National Gardens Scheme; www.ngs.org.uk/.
• Peter Pan Moat Brae Trust, Moat Brae, George Street, Dumfries DG1 2EA; www.peterpanmoatbrae.org/.
• Dylan Thomas; www.dylanthomasboathouse.com/ and www.dylanthomas.com/.

Sources of Quotes

Page number in left column refers to the position of the relevant quotation in this edition of *A Writer's Garden*.

6   Elizabeth von Arnim, *Elizabeth and Her German Garden*, Virago, 1985, page 52.

8   Elizabeth von Arnim, *Elizabeth and Her German Garden*, Virago, 1985, page 33.

10   Jane Austen, *Sense and Sensibility*, Penguin Popular Classics, 1994, page 295.

12   Letter, Jane Austen to Cassandra Austen, 18 December 1798, in Deidre Le Faye (ed.), *Jane Austen's Letters*, Oxford University Press, 2011, page 29.

12   Letter, Jane Austen to Cassandra Austen, 15 June 1808, in Deidre Le Faye (ed.), *Jane Austen's Letters*, Oxford University Press, 2011, page 132.

16   Letter, Jane Austen to Cassandra Austen, 31 May 1811, in Deidre Le Faye (ed.), *Jane Austen's Letters*, Oxford University Press, 2011, page 200.

18   Letter, Jane Austen to Francis Austen, 3 July 1813, in Deidre Le Faye (ed.), *Jane Austen's Letters*, Oxford University Press, 2011, page 224.

20   Rupert Brooke, 'The Old Vicarage, Grantchester (Café des Westens, Berlin, May 1912)', in Geoffrey Keynes (ed.), *The Poetical Works of Rupert Brooke,* Faber, 1960, page 67.

20, 22   Letter, Rupert Brooke to Noël Olivier, July 1909, in *The History of the Orchard Grantchester*, Rupert Brooke Society / The Orchard Grantchester, n.d. © Estate of Rupert Brooke and reprinted by permission of Faber and Faber Ltd.

23   Rupert Brooke, 'The Old Vicarage, Grantchester (Café des Westens, Berlin, May 1912)', in Geoffrey Keynes (ed.), *The Poetical Works of Rupert Brooke,* Faber, 1960, page 69.

25   Ibid., page 67.

27   Rupert Brooke, 'Sonnet 1914, V. The Soldier', in Geoffrey Keynes (ed.), *The Poetical Works of Rupert Brooke,* Faber, 1960, page 23.

28   Letter, John Ruskin to Thomas Carlyle, Denmark Hill, Monday, 23 October 1871. Letter in the collection of the Brantwood Trust; www.brantwood.org.uk.

32   John Ruskin, *Proserpina: Studies of Wayside Flowers*, Vol. II, George Allen, 1877, IV *Giulietta*.

32   John Ruskin, *Proserpina: Studies of Wayside Flowers*, Vol. II, George Allen, 1877, I *Viola*.

35   John Ruskin, *Unto This Last, Four Essays on the First Principles of Political Economy: IV Ad Valorem,* Cornhill Magazine, 1860.

36   Agatha Christie, *An Autobiography*, Harper Collins, 1993, page 20. Reprinted by permission of Harper Collins Publishers Ltd (© 1977).

36   Ibid., page 525.

37   Agatha Christie, *Dead Man's Folly,* Harper, 2002, page 15. Reprinted by permission of Harper Collins Publishers Ltd. (© 1956).

40   Mathew Prichard, *National Trust Guide to Greenway*, National Trust, 2006, page 3.

40   Agatha Christie, *An Autobiography*, Harper Collins, 1993, page 549. Reprinted by permission of Harper Collins Publishers Ltd (© 1977).

40   Agatha Christie, *Five Little Pigs*, Harper, 2007, page 138. Reprinted by permission of Harper Collins Publishers Ltd. (© 1942).

45   Letter, Beatrix Potter to Millie Warne, 30 September 1906, in Judy Taylor (ed.), *Beatrix Potter's Letters*, Frederick Warne, 1989.

47   Letter, Beatrix Potter to Millie Warne, 6 September 1906, in Judy Taylor (ed.), *Beatrix Potter's Letters*, Frederick Warne, 1989.

54   Roald Dahl, *The Minpins*, Puffin Books, 2008, page 48.

60   W.B. Yeats, 'Among School Children' in *The Tower*, Macmillan, 1928.

62 Letter, Charles Dickens to Chandos Wren Hoskyns, 15 December 1858, in Graham Storey and Kathleen Tillotson (eds), *Letters of Charles Dickens*, Vol. 8: 1856–1858, Clarendon Press, 1995, page 722. By permission of Oxford University Press.

66 Letter, Charles Dickens to Mrs Annie Fields, 25 May 1868, in Graham Storey, Margaret Brown and Kathleen Tillotson (eds), *Letters of Charles Dickens*, Vol. 12: 1868–1870, Clarendon Press, 2002, page 119. By permission of Oxford University Press.

68 Virginia Woolf, 3 July 1919, in Quentin Bell, Angelica Garnett and Anne Olivier Bell (eds), *Selected Diaries of Virginia Woolf*, Vintage, 2008, page 83. Reprinted by permission of The Random House Group Ltd.

68 Ibid.

72 Ibid., page 267.

76 Letter, Winston Churchill to Stanley Baldwin, 7 September 1925, WSC/Baldwin 7 September 1925, Churchill Papers 18/11, Churchill Archive, Cambridge. Reproduced with permission of Curtis Brown, London on behalf of the Estate of Sir Winston S. Churchill. © Winston S. Churchill.

78 Ibid.

81 Letter, Winston Churchill to Clementine Churchill, 2 September 1923, WSC/CC 2 September 1923, Spencer-Churchill Papers, Churchill Archive, Cambridge. Reproduced with permission of Curtis Brown, London on behalf of the Estate of Sir Winston S. Churchill. © Winston S. Churchill.

85 Laurence Sterne, *The Life and Opinions of Tristram Shandy, Gentleman,* dedication to 2nd edn 1760. Courtesy of the Laurence Sterne Trust.

92 George Bernard Shaw, *Bernard Shaw's Rhyming Picture Guide to Ayot St Lawrence*, Leagrave Press, 1950, page 16. Courtesy of The Society of Authors, on behalf of the Bernard Shaw Estate.

99 Ted Hughes, 'Lumb Chimneys', in Paul Keegan (ed.), *Ted Hughes Collected Poems*, Faber & Faber, 2005, page 457. © Estate of Ted Hughes and reprinted by permission of Faber and Faber Ltd.

106 Henry James, *The Awkward Age*, Penguin Modern Classics, 1966, page 245.

108 E.F. Benson, 'Miss Mapp', in *The Complete Mapp & Lucia*, Vol. 1, Wordsworth Classics, 2011, page 241.

111 E.F. Benson, Preface to the 1922 edn of 'Miss Mapp', in *The Complete Mapp & Lucia*, Vol. 1, Wordsworth Classics, 2011, page 239.

114 John Clare, 'Emmonsale's Heath', in *The Rural Muse*, Forgotten Books Classic Reprint Series, 2012, page 48.

118 Ibid., page 47.

120 Thomas Hardy, 'Domicilium', in James Gibson (ed.), *Chosen Poems of Thomas Hardy*, The Thomas Hardy Society, page 29.

124 Thomas Hardy, *Under The Greenwood Tree*, Wordsworth Classics, 2004, page 3.

130 Letter, Robert Burns to Alexander Cunningham, 27 July 1788, Friends of Ellisland; www.ellislandfarm.co.uk/.

135 Robert Burns, 'Verses in Friars' Carse Hermitage', in James A. Mackay (ed.), *Robert Burns: The Complete Poetical Works*, Alloway Publishing, 1993, page 324.

139 William Wordsworth, *The Prelude, Book 1*, Penguin Classics, 1995, page 52.

145 William Wordsworth, 'Ode on Intimations of Immortality from Recollections of Early Childhood', in *The Poetical Works of William Wordsworth*, Routledge, Warne & Routledge, 1863, page 266.

149 Letter, Walter Scott to Daniel Terry, September 1812, in H.J.C. Grierson et al., *The Letters of Sir Walter Scott*, Vol. 3, Constable, 1932–7, pages 153–5.

158 Rudyard Kipling, 'The Glory of the Garden', in *The Complete Verse*, Kyle Cathie, 1990, page 604.

167 Ibid.

Further Reading

Archer, Mary, *The Story of the Old Vicarage Grantchester*, The Old Vicarage Press, 2012; www.jeffreyarcher.co.uk

Bate, Jonathan, *John Clare A Biography*, Picador, 2004

Davies, Hunter, *William Wordsworth*, Frances Lincoln, 2009

Dearden, James S., *Brantwood: The Story of John Ruskin's Coniston Home*, The Ruskin Foundation, 2009

Denyer, Susan, *At Home with Beatrix Potter*, Frances Lincoln in association with the National Trust, 2009

Hancock, Nuala, *Gardens in the Work of Virginia Woolf*, Bloomsbury Heritage Series, Cecil Woolf Publishers, 2005

Holroyd, Michael, *Bernard Shaw: The One-Volume Definitive Edition*, Chatto & Windus, 1997

Jackson, Kevin, *The Worlds of John Ruskin*, Pallas Athene & The Ruskin Foundation, 2011

Lear, Linda, *Beatrix Potter – The Extraordinary Life of a Victorian Genius*, Penguin, 2008

Lee, Hermione, *Virginia Woolf*, Vintage, 1997

Sturrock, Donald, *Storyteller – The Life of Roald Dahl*, Harper Press, 2011

Thompson, Laura, *Agatha Christie – An English Mystery*, Headline Review, 2008

Tomalin, Claire, *Charles Dickens, A Life*, Penguin, 2012

Tomalin, Claire, *Jane Austen, A Life*, Penguin, 2012

Tomalin, Claire, *Thomas Hardy: The Time-Torn Man*, Penguin, 2012

Watts, Alan S., *Dickens at Gad's Hill*, Cedric Dickens and Elvendon Press, 1989

Westwood, Peter J., *Jean Armour – Mrs Robert Burns*, Creedon Publications, 1996

Wilson, Kim, *In the Garden with Jane Austen*, Frances Lincoln, 2009

Index

Readers' Note: Captions to illustrations are indicated by *italic page numbers*.

A

Abbotsford *9*, 9, *148*, 148–57, *150–51*, *152*
Abercrombie's Practical Gardener 114
achilleas *92*
agapanthus *148*, *155*, 155
Ailsworth Heath *118*, *119*
alkanet *25*
alliums *55*, *69*
alpine gardens: Gipsy House *58*, 60
amaranthus *163*
anemones 12, *14*, *110*
apples *24*, *123*, 127, *142*, *143*, 145, 155
arcades *89*
Archer, Dame Mary 20, *23*, 26
Archer, Lord (Jeffrey) 20, *23*, 25
Armour, Jean 130, 132, 136
Arvon Foundation 104
Ashfield 36
Auld Lang Syne 132, *133*, 136
Austen, Cassandra (sister) 10, 12, 14, 18
Austen, Edward (brother) 10, 12, 16, 18, *19*
Austen, Henry (brother) 10, 18
Austen, Jane 6, 10–19, *12*
Austen, Reverend (father) 10, 14
Awkward Age, The 106
azaleas *30*, *52*, *53*

B

Bambridge, Elsie *see* Kipling, Elsie
Bambridge, George 167
Barber, Charles 64
Barrie, J.M. 8
Bartholomew, Marie 71

Bartholomew, Percy 71
Bateman's *158–9*, 158–67, *160*
Bates, H.E. 6
Batsford, Sir Brian 113
Battery, The 40, *40–41*
beans 140
beehives 71, *74*
Bell, Vanessa 68
Benson, E.F. 106–13, *111*
Bentigh 12, *13*
Bernard Shaw's Rhyming Picture Guide 97
BFG, The 60
bird houses *70*
Blenheim Palace 6, 76, 78
bluebells *43*
Blyton, Enid 8, 8
boathouse
    Greenway 6, 42, *43*
    Laugharne 6, *7*
Bogie, William 153
borage *143*
Boscombe House 8
bowling green: Monk's House 71
brachyglottis *91*
Brantwood 9, 28–35, *29*, *30*
Bride of Lammermoor, The 157
Brooke, Rupert *20*, 20–27, *22*
Brunt, George 64, *65*
Burghley House 114
Burnett, Frances Hodgson 8
Burn's Night 137
Burns, Roberts 6, 130–37, *132*
Bus Conductor, The 113

C

Calder Valley *98*, 99, *100–01*, *104*, 105
calendulas *122*
Callan, Robin 24
camellias 42

THE WRITER'S GARDEN

campsis 110
caravan: Gipsy House 58, *59*
Carlyon family 39
Carpenter, T. Edward 18
Castle Cottage 48, *50–51, 52*
Celebrated Jumping Frog of Calaveras County, The 7
Charlie and the Chocolate Factory 60
Chartwell 6, 76–83, *77, 78*
Chawton House 14–19, *15, 18*
Chawton House Library 19
cherry blossom *24*
Cherry-Garrard, Apsley 94, *96*
chestnut trees *91*
Christie, Agatha 36–43, *40, 43*
Churchill, Clementine (wife) 76, *76*
Churchill, Mary (daughter) 76, 78
Churchill, Sir Winston 6, *76*, 76–83, *83*
Clare, John 6, 114–19, *116*
Cock and Bull Story, A 88
Cockermouth *see* Wordsworth House
Colden Water 99, *100–01*, 103
conservatories
   Abbotsford *156*
   Gad's Hill Place 65, 66, *67*
   Max Gate 128
   Monk's House 72
containers *70, 72*
Cox, Ka 22
crocosmia *123*, 128, *129*
Crosland, Felicity 60, 61

D

Dahl, Olivia (daughter) 58
Dahl, Roald 6, 7, 54–61, *57*
Dahl, Theo (son) 58
dahlias 155, *155*
daisy, shasta 110, *123*
Danny The Champion of the World 59, 60
Darnell, Dorothy and Beatrix 18
Dart, river *38*
David Copperfield 63
Dead Man's Folly 37, *43*
Derwent, river *138*

Dickens, Charles 7, 62–7, *66*
Dickens, Charley (son) 66–7
Dickens, Katey (daughter) 64, 66
Dickens, Mamie (daughter) 65
Dickinson, Emily 6
Dove Cottage *144, 146*, 145–7
Drake, Sir Francis 39
Draper, Eliza 88
Drury, Fred 94
du Maurier, Daphne 6
Dudwell, river 163, *164*

E

Elizabeth and Her German Garden 7–8
Ellisland 130–37, *131, 133, 134*
elm trees 71, 75
Elton, Edward 39
Emmonsale's 114, *118*, 118
environmentalism 32, 117
Esio Trot 60
Everett, John *126*

F

Fairfax, John 99, 103
Fantastic Mr Fox 60
Far from the Madding Crowd 125
farming 132, 136, 164, 167
fern garden: Brantwood 35
ferns 34, *35*, 65
Ferns of the English Lake Country, The 35
fish *79*
Fitzwilliams of Milton Hall 116, 117
Five Little Pigs 40
follies
   Ellisland *135*
   The Old Vicarage 20, *23*
Friars' Carse *134*, 135, *135*, 136, 137
Friends of Ellisland 137

G

Gabriel (gardener) 111
Gad's Hill Place *62*, 62–7, *63, 65*

Gammon, George 110
Gardener's Dictionary, The 140
geraniums
   hardy *53*, 53, *103*, 103, 117
   see also pelargoniums
Gifford, Emma *see* Hardy, Emma
Gill, Eric 25, *27*
ginkgo 72
Gipsy House *54*, 54–61
glasshouses *see* conservatories
Godden, Rumer 113
Godmersham Park 10–14, *14*
Godwin, Fay *98*, 104
Grahame, Kenneth 8
Grant, Duncan 22
Granta, river 21
Grantchester 20–7
Grasmere *see* Dove Cottage
Gravel Walk (Chawton House) 15, 16
Great Expectations 65
Great Maytham Hall 8
Great Missenden 54, 56, 57
Green Hedges 8, *8*
greenhouses *see* conservatories
Greenshields, John 153
Greenway 6, *36–7*, 36–43
Gremlins 54, 56
Guardian Hare sculpture *27*
Gunnera manicata 165

H

Haggard, H. Rider 164
Hardy, Emma 125, 127–8
Hardy, Florence (2nd wife) *127*, 128
Hardy, Thomas 6, 7, 120–29, *127*
Hardy's Cottage *1, 120–21*, 120–25, *124, 129*
Harvey, Richard 39
Heelis, Beatrix *see* Potter, Beatrix
Heelis, William (husband) 48, 53
Helpston *114*, 114–19, *115, 118*
Henderson, Joseph 116
herbs 140
Hermitage, The *135*, 135

Hicks, Rosalind and Anthony 39
Higgs, Henry 94
Hill Top Farm *9*, 44–53
History of the English-Speaking Peoples 78
Hogarth, William 86
honeysuckle 128
horse chestnuts 25
Hughes, Carol 99, 104
Hughes, Ted 98–105, *99, 104*
Hutchison, Mary 147
Hyde, H. Montgomery 113

I

insect 'hotel' *129*
irises *47*
iron railings *91*
Italianate gardens
   Godmersham 12
   Lumb Bank *103*, 103
   Monk's House 68, *72*, 75

J

James and the Giant Peach 6, 58
James, Henry 106–13, *111*
Jane Austen Memorial Trust 18
Jane Austen Society 18
Jane Austen's House Museum 14
John Clare Trust 119
Jungle Books, The 160

K

Kew Gardens 6
Kipling, Carrie (wife) 158–67
Kipling, Elsie (daughter) 164, 167
Kipling, John (son) 164
Kipling, John Lockwood (father) 158
Kipling, Josephine (daughter) 158
Kipling, Rudyard 158–67
kitchen gardens
   Abbotsford 149, 153, 155
   Bateman's *161*, 163

kitchen gardens (*cont.*)
 Brantwood 32, *33*
 Chartwell 78, 79, 81
 Chawton House 15, 18
 Ellisland 137
 Gad's Hill Place 64
 Greenway 39
 Hardy's Cottage 123
 Helpston 114
 Hill Top Farm *45*, 47, *49*, *53*, 53
 Lumb Bank 103
 Max Gate *126*, 127, 128
 Monk's House 71, *74*, 75
 Shandy Hall 86
 Shaw's Corner 94, *96*, 96
 Wordsworth House 140, 141, *142*, 145
Knight family 12
 Edward Knight *see* Austen, Edward (brother)
 John Knight *19*
 Montagu Knight 18

L

Lady of the Lake, The 157
lakes: Chartwell 6, 78
Lamb House 106–13, *106–07*, *108*
Lamb Players, The 113
landscape gardens 14
Laurence Sterne Trust 88
Lawrence, T.E. 94
Lee, Herman 128
Lefroy, Tom 12
Leigh, Vivien 94
Lerner, Sandy 19
Life and Opinions of Tristram Shandy, Gentleman, The 85, 86, 90
lilac *25*, *53*
lime tree avenues
 Bateman's 161
 Gipsy House *55*, 61
 Godmersham 12, *13*
Linden, Estrid *23*
Linton, William James 35

Little Whitefield *see* Gipsy House
Lloyd, Martha 14
Lumb Bank *98*, 98–105, *100–01*, *102*
Lutyens, Edwin 18

M

McCrum, Bridget *43*
magnolias 39, *42*
Mallowan, Max 36, 39–40, *40*
Mansfield Park 14, 16
Mapp and Lucia novels 110, 111, *112*
Marlborough Pavilion *81*, 81
Max Gate 6, 125–9, *126*
Maxwell Scott *see* Scott
Mayor of Casterbridge, The 125
maze: Gipsy House *60*, 61
Memories with Food at Gipsy House 61
mill 163–4, *164*
Moat Brae 8, *9*
Moat, John 99, 103
Modern Painters 28
Monkman, Kenneth and Julia 88
Monk's House *4–5*, *68*, 68–75, *73*
Montagu, Venetia 81
Moorland Garden 32
Morris Garden 153, 157
Mossgiel 137
moths 90
Motion, Andrew 104
Mrs Dalloway 6
mulberry tree *108*, 110, 163
Mysterious Affair at Styles, The 42
Mystery of Edwin Drood, The 65, 67

N

Naismyth, Alexander *132*
Neal, Patricia 56, 60
Near Sawrey *4–5*, 45, 48, *50–51*, *52*, 53
Neeve, Henry 22

Northanger Abbey 10, 19
Not a Penny More, Not a Penny Less 25

O

Old Vicarage, The (Grantchester) 20–27, *22*
Olivier, Noël 20, 22
Orchard House (Grantchester) 20, 24
orchards
 Bateman's *161*, 161, *162*, 167
 Chartwell 79
 Ellisland *133*
 Gad's Hill Place 64
 Gipsy House 58
 Grantchester *see* Orchard House (Grantchester)
 Hardy's Cottage 123
 Hill Top Farm 47, *53*
 Max Gate 128
 Monk's House 72, *74*, 75
 Shandy Hall 88
 Shaw's Corner *96*, 96
orchids 60
Our Mutual Friend 65

P

painting studio *78*, 79
Parsons, Trekkie Ritchie 73
Parsons, Alfred 109–10
paths *123*, *158*, *163*
pears 161, *162*
Pearson, Chris 91
pelargoniums 64–5, *67*, *122*
peonies *47*
Peter Pan 8
Peter Pan Moat Brae Trust 8
phlomis *156*
Pickwick Papers 63
Plath, Sylvia 99
plums *118*
Poems, Chiefly in the Scottish Dialect 130

Poems, Descriptive of Rural Life and Scenery 116
ponds
 Bateman's 164, *166*, 167
 Chartwell *79*
 Greenway *43*
 Monk's House *72*
Poor Man and the Lady, The 123, 125
poppies 28, *30*, 34, 58, *69*, 94
Potter, Beatrix *2–3*, 6, 7, 44–53, *48*
potting sheds *129*
Prichard, Mathew 40
Pride and Prejudice 10, 12, 16, 18, 19
Professor's Garden, The 31
Puck of Pook's Hill 160, 163–4, 167
Purdie, Tom 155–6
Pygmalion 93

R

red campion *25*
Remains of Elmet 99, 104
Repton, Humphry 14
Return of the Native, The 125
Rewards and Fairies 160, 167
rhododendrons *42*, 52
Riddell, Robert *134*, 134
Roald Dahl Museum and Story Centre 57
rose gardens
 Bateman's 164
 Chartwell 81, *82*, 83
 Godmersham 12
 Shaw's Corner *95*
roses 67, 68, 70, 73, 80–81, *82*, 90, 95, 142, *143*, 164, *166*
Rupert Brooke Museum/Society 24
Rural Muse, The 118
Ruskin, John 28–35, *32*
Rye *106*, 106, 110, *111*, 111, *112*

S

Saint Joan 93
St Mary's Church, Rye *108*

St Nicholas Church, Chawton *18*, 18

saxifrages 7, *47*

Scots Musical Museum, The 132

Scott, Charlotte (granddaughter) 156

Scott, Charlotte (wife) 6, 155, 156

Scott, Dame Jean Maxwell 157

Scott, Mary Monica (great-granddaughter) 157

Scott, Mrs Patricia Maxwell 157

Scott, Sir Walter 7, 148–57, *149*

Scott, Major General Sir Walter Maxwell 157

Secret Garden, The 8

Sense and Sensibility 10, 15, 16, 19

Sentimental Journey, A 88

Severn, Joan and Arthur 31, 32

Shakespeare, William 65

Shandy Hall *84*, 84–91, *86, 87, 89*

Shaw, Charlotte (wife) 93–4

Shaw, George Bernard 7, 92–7

Shaw's Corner *92*, 92–7, *95*

Shelley, Percy Bysshe 8

Shepherd's Calender, The 116

shrubberies
  Chawton House 15, 16
  Gad's Hill Place 64

statuary *43, 58, 74, 94, 95, 116, 153*

Stephens, Berty 127

Sterne, Elizabeth (wife) 86

Sterne, Laurence 84–91, *85*

Stevenson, Mrs 24

Steventon *10*, 10

Stoneleigh 14

Stones of Venice 28

Story of The Old Vicarage, Grantchester, The 20

summer houses
  Chartwell 81
  The Old Vicarage 20, *22*
  Wordsworth House 145, *146*

sundial 164, *166*

sweet peas *91*, 140

swimming pools
  Chartwell *79, 79*
  Godmersham 12

Swiss cottages
  Gad's Hill Place 63, 64, *64*, 67
  The Old Vicarage 20

T

Tale of Johnny Town-mouse, The 48

Tale of Peter Rabbit, The 47

Tale of Samuel Whiskers, The 48

Tale of the Flopsy Bunnies, The 47

Tale of Two Cities, A 65

'Tam O' Shanter: A Tale' *134*

Tam O' Shanter Walk, The 135, 137

Temple, The (Godmersham) *13*

Ternan, Ellen 65

Terrace, The 142

Terry, Elizabeth 149

Thomas, Dylan 7

Thoreau, Henry David 7

Tilden, Philip 78, 79, 81

Tomlin, Stephen *75*

topiary: Godmersham 12, *14*

Topp, Chris *91*

Town End *see* Dove Cottage

Tristram Shandy see Life and Opinions of Tristram Shandy, Gentleman

Turn of the Screw, The 113

Twain, Mark 7

U

Uncommercial Traveller, The 63

Under the Greenwood Tree 120, *124*, 125, 127, 128

V

Valon, Annette 145

vegetable gardens *see* kitchen gardens

verbena *156*

veronicastrum *92*

Village Minstrel, The 116

von Arnim, Elizabeth, 6, 7–8

Voyage Out, The 68

W

Walden 7

walled gardens
  Abbotsford 153, *155*
  Bateman's 161, *163*
  Chawton House 16, 18
  Gipsy House 61
  Godmersham 12
  Greenway 39, 42
  Lamb House 113
  Lumb Bank *103*, 103
  Wordsworth House 140, *141, 143*

walnut tree 110

War Sonnets, 1914 25, 27

Warne, Millie 47

Warne, Norman 45

water features
  Bateman's 164
  Chartwell 76, 79
  see also ponds

Waverley 157

Widnall, Page 20

Wild Garden, The 32

wild gardens/wilderness
  Bateman's 163
  Chawton House *17*
  Gad's Hill Place 64
  Shandy Hall *90*

Wildgust, Patrick 91

Williams, Charles 39

Wind in the Willows, The 8

Winsten, Stephen and Clare *94*

Winterbrook House 36

wisteria *27, 46*

woodland gardens 7
  Abbotsford 155–6
  Bateman's 164
  Ellisland Farm 137
  Greenway 40
  Hardy's Cottage *124, 125*
  Max Gate 127, 128

Woodlanders, The 127

Woolf, Leonard (husband) 68–75, *69, 74*

Woolf, Virginia *4–5*, 6, 7, 22, 68–75, *69, 71, 72, 73, 74, 75*

Wordsworth, Dorothy (sister) 139, 147

Wordsworth, William 8, 138–47

Wordsworth House 140–45

Worst Journey in the World, The 96

writing huts/rooms *6–7, 6–7*
  Gad's Hill Place *64, 64, 66*, 67
  Gipsy House 57, *57*, 58
  Lamb House 111
  Monk's House *4–5, 71*, 71
  Shaw's Corner *97*

Y

yews 153

Z

Zig-Zaggy (Brantwood) 31

Acknowledgments

Author's and Photographer's Acknowledgments

The author and photographer would like warmly to thank the following organizations and individuals for their help with this book:

Arvon Foundation; Charles Dickens Centre (Gad's Hill) Limited; Chawton House Library; Friars Carse Hotel; Friends of Ellisland; Gad's Hill School; Godmersham Park Estate; Jane Austen's House Museum; John Clare Trust; Peter Pan Moat Brae Trust; The Brantwood Trust; The Laurence Sterne Trust; The National Trust; The Orchard, Grantchester; The Plant Specialist, Great Missenden; The Roald Dahl Museum and Story Centre; The Rupert Brooke Society; The Wordsworth Trust.

Special thanks to: Alan Bird and Sarah Parry at Chawton House Library; Allison Pritchard and Nicholas Dickenson at Monk's House; Carol Hughes; Carrie Taylor and Catherine Kay at Dove Cottage; Cathy Agnew at the Peter Pan Moat Brae Trust; Colin Clark and Sabina Collier at Greenway; David Dykes at John Clare Cottage; Edward Allwright; Mrs Felicity Dahl and Wendy Kress at Gipsy House; Greg Ellis and Steve Barton at Godmersham Park; Ilona Leighton-Goodall; Isabel Snowden and Ann Channon at Jane Austen's House Museum; Jennifer Ide; Karen Finlay, Billy Hughes and Matthew Withey at Abbotsford; Kirsty Fairhead and Amanda Thackeray at Wordsworth's House and Garden; Len Bernamont at Bateman's; Les Byers and Ronnie Cairns at Ellisland; Liz MacFarlane, Joanna Hudson and Pete Tasker at Hill Top; Lizzie Dunford at Shaw's Corner; Lorna Beckett at the Rupert Brooke Society; Mandy Marshall; Dame Mary Archer, Rachael Avery and Paula Morrin at The Old Vicarage; Nigel Wilkinson; Patrick Wildgust and Chris Pearson at Shandy Hall; Rachel Stokes, Jennifer Davis and Harriet Still at Hardy's Cottage and Max Gate; Rachel White at the Roald Dahl Museum and Story Centre; Sally Beamish, Rachel Litton and Helen Wharton at Brantwood; Sue Higginson, Sean Walter and Keith Pounder at The Plant Specialist; Susannah Mayor and Mr and Mrs Patrick Rogers at Lamb House; Tracey Willis and Giles Palmer at Chartwell.

And to Helen Griffin of Frances Lincoln; James Wills at Watson Little; designer Anne Wilson; editor Joanna Chisholm; proofreader Annelise Evans; Jake Bennett; and indexer Michèle Clarke for their professional support.

Picture Acknowledgments

All photographs by Richard Hanson except: Mark William Penny/Shutterstock, 7l; John Gittens/Shutterstock, 7r; Enid Blyton Society/Seven Stories 8; Graeme Robertson/Courtesy of the Peter Pan Moat Brae Trust 9tl; Jane Austen's House Museum, Jane Austen Memorial Trust: 10, 12, 15t; Joe Low/Jane Austen's House Museum, Jane Austen Memorial Trust: 19; Michael Nicholson/Corbis: 20; The Rupert Brooke Society: 22 tr; T.A. & J. Green of Grasmere, courtesy of Brantwood Trust: 32; Popperfoto/Getty Images: 40, 43; © National Trust: 48; © National Trust/Reece Winsten: 94; Felicity Dahl, courtesy of The Roald Dahl Museum and Story Centre: 57t; Bettmann/Corbis: 66b, 111l, 111c, 132; S.L. Fildes 1871 sketch/Corbis: 66t; Frank Scherschel/Time Life Pictures/Getty Images: 83; Laurence Sterne Trust: 85br, 86l, 88; © estate of Fay Godwin, c/o British Library/National Portrait Gallery, London: 99; REX features/British Library: 105; Hulton-Deutsch Collection/Corbis: 111r; Thomas Hardy Archive and Collection, Dorset County Museum: 126l; E.O. Hoppe/Corbis: 127; Georgios Kollidas/Shutterstock 147; Nicku/Shutterstock 149, 167; front cover Fiona McLeod.